CHRISTOPHER CARSTENS, DENIS McNAMARA, and ALEXIS KUTARNA

SOLEMNITIES

CELEBRATING A TAPESTRY
OF DIVINE BEAUTY

ASCENSION

West Chester, Pennsylvania

Excerpts from the English translation of the *Catechism of the Catholic Church* for use in the United States of America © 1994 United States Catholic Conference, Inc.–Libreria Editrice Vaticana. Used with permission. English translation of the *Catechism of the Catholic Church: Modifications from the Editio Typica* © 1997 United States Conference of Catholic Bishops–Libreria Editrice Vaticana.

Unless otherwise noted, Scripture passages are from the Revised Standard Version–Second Catholic Edition © 2006 by the Division of Christian Education of the National Council of the Churches of Christ in the United States of America. Used by permission. All rights reserved.

Ascension
PO Box 1990
West Chester, PA 19380
1-800-376-0520

ascensionpress.com

Cover design: Rosemary Strohm

Printed in the United States of America
22 23 24 25 26 5 4 3 2 1

ISBN 978-1-954881-60-0 (hardcover)

CONTENTS

List of Illustrations iv

Introduction 1

The Immaculate Conception of the Blessed Virgin Mary 2

The Nativity of the Lord (Christmas) 8

Mary, the Holy Mother of God 14

The Epiphany of the Lord 20

St. Joseph, Spouse of the Blessed Virgin Mary 26

The Annunciation of the Lord 32

Easter 38

The Ascension of the Lord 44

Pentecost Sunday 50

The Most Holy Trinity 56

The Most Holy Body and Blood of Christ (Corpus Christi) 62

The Most Sacred Heart of Jesus 68

The Nativity of St. John the Baptist 74

Saints Peter and Paul, Apostles 80

The Assumption of the Blessed Virgin Mary 86

All Saints 92

Our Lord Jesus Christ, King of the Universe (Christ the King) 98

About the Authors 104

Notes 105

LIST OF ILLUSTRATIONS

Francisco de Zurbarán, *The Immaculate Conception*, 1628–1630, oil on canvas, 128 cm x 89 cm (P002992). Madrid, Museo Nacional del Prado. © Photographic Archive Museo Nacional del Prado

The Mystic Nativity, Sandro Botticelli, 1500, National Gallery, London

Madonna in the Church, Jan Van Eyck, 1428, Gemäldegalerie, State Museum, Berlin

Adoration of the Magi, Domenico Ghirlandaio, 1488, Oespedale degli Innocenti, Florence

Marriage of the Virgin, Pietro Perugino, c. 1500–1515, Musée de Beaux-Arts, Caen

Murate Annunciation, Fra Filippo Lippi, c. 1440–1445, Alte Pinakothek, Munich

The Resurrection of Christ, Raphael, c. 1499–1502, São Paulo Museum of Art, São Paulo, Brazil

The Ascension of Christ, Benjamin West, 1801, Denver Art Museum

Pentecost, folio 79 from the *Très Riches Heures du Duc de Berry*, Jean Colombe, c. 1485–1490, Musée Condé, Chantilly, France

Central Panel, Mural at the Cathedral of the Madeleine, Felix Lieftuchter, c. 1918, Salt Lake City

The Mass of Saint Gregory the Great, anonymous, c. 1500, Groeningemuseum, Bruges

The Sacred Heart of Jesus, central panel of a three-part mural, Leonard Porter, 2004, Cathedral of St. Joseph, Sioux Falls, South Dakota

The Birth and Naming of John the Baptist, from the Saint John Altarpiece, Rogier Van der Weyden, c. 1454, Gemäldegalerie, Berlin

Icon of the Embrace of the Apostles Peter and Paul, Angelos Akotantos, c. 1436–1450, The Ashmolean Museum of Art and Archaeology, Oxford

The Assumption of the Virgin, Ambrogio da Fossano (known as Bergognone), c. 1522, oil and gold on wood. Metropolitan Museum of Art, New York

The Trinity in Its Glory from the *Hours of Étienne Chevalier*, Jean Fouquet, c. 1452, Musée Condé, Chantilly, France

Christ in Majesty from the *Last Judgment Mosaic*, artist unknown, thirteenth century, Baptistery, Florence

Introduction

*This is the day which the L*ORD* has made; let us rejoice and be glad in it.*
–Psalm 118:24

Not all days are created equal. Mother's Day, the Fourth of July, Presidents' Day, Thanksgiving, birthdays, and wedding anniversaries all play an important role in the lives of Americans. Some of these celebrations are national holidays, while others are more personal. Regardless of their scope, certain days every year rise above others.

The same is true in the life of the Church. Certain days are set aside because they commemorate important events, persons, or beliefs. For this reason, the Church holds up these days for special reverence, celebrating, for example, the annunciation of the angel Gabriel to Mary, the resurrection of Jesus on Easter, the nativity of St. John the Baptist, the universal sovereignty of Christ the King, and Mary's bodily assumption into heaven.

Like federal holidays or regularly scheduled family reunions, the Church has its own way of ranking and observing the days of her year. The first type of liturgical celebration that rises above the "common" weekday are *optional memorials*, such as that of St. Blaise on February 3, followed by the *memorials*, which are required to be observed, such as that of St. Francis of Assisi on October 4. Next in order of importance, *feasts* hold an even higher ranking, since their subjects carry a greater significance in the life of the universal Church, such as the Nativity of the Blessed Virgin Mary on September 8. At the top of the list, second only to Sunday in their importance, are the Church's *solemnities*.

In the Roman rite of the Church, there are seventeen solemnities observed over the course of the year. Some commemorate the most prominent among the saints, such as St. John the Baptist and St. Joseph. Others bring to our minds and hearts great truths of our Faith, such as the Holy Eucharist on *Corpus Christi* (the Body and Blood of Christ), the nativity of our Lord on Christmas, and Jesus' ascension into heaven. Some solemnities have the Blessed Virgin Mary as their subject, such as the Immaculate Conception and the Assumption. Here are the seventeen solemnities celebrated in the Roman rite:

1. The Immaculate Conception of the Blessed Virgin Mary
2. The Nativity of the Lord (Christmas)
3. Mary, the Holy Mother of God
4. The Epiphany of the Lord
5. St. Joseph, Spouse of the Blessed Virgin Mary
6. The Annunciation of the Lord
7. Easter
8. The Ascension of the Lord
9. Pentecost Sunday
10. The Most Holy Trinity
11. The Most Holy Body and Blood of Christ (*Corpus Christi*)
12. The Most Sacred Heart of Jesus
13. The Nativity of St. John the Baptist
14. Saints Peter and Paul, Apostles
15. The Assumption of the Blessed Virgin Mary
16. All Saints
17. Our Lord Jesus Christ, King of the Universe (Christ the King)

As followers of Christ, observing these great solemnities should fill us with joy and hope. We should not be fooled by thinking that "solemnity" means we should act "solemn," as in gloomy, serious, or sad. The solemnities of the Church are more appropriately celebrated as sacred, sublime, awe-inspiring, and—above all—joyful!

The layout of this book seeks to demonstrate the glory of these sublime days. Each entry begins with the liturgical, biblical, and spiritual substance proper to each celebration. Next, each chapter features a beautiful work of art from the tradition, accompanied by a descriptive commentary on each piece. Finally, every chapter concludes with insights about how a particular solemnity can come to life, not simply in the liturgy or on canvas, but in the hearts and homes of believers.

It is our sincere hope that this book, *Solemnities: Celebrating a Tapestry of Divine Beauty*, be a source of prayer, beauty, and divine life for all who read it. More importantly, may each of these great celebrations be a source of great joy and holiness for you in the year ahead.

The Immaculate Conception
of the Blessed Virgin Mary

December 8

The Church's liturgical year begins on the first Sunday of Advent, which falls in late November or early December. Not long after this holy cycle starts, the Church observes the Solemnity of the Immaculate Conception of the Blessed Virgin Mary on December 8. On this first feast of the liturgical year, the Church shows us how Mary's singular grace applies to each of us.

Here is one way to understand the meaning of the Immaculate Conception. When someone falls into a deep, potentially deadly pit, we seek to rescue him from it. This is what Christ does for us in Baptism—he rescues us from the deadly pit of original sin and infuses our souls with his sanctifying grace. But one person—Mary—was saved by Christ before her very conception; she was kept from falling into the pit entirely. In either case, through rescue or prevention, we all need saving, and Jesus is the one who does it.

Pius IX, who served as pope from 1846 to 1878, promulgated the dogma of the Immaculate Conception in 1854, and thereby made official the Church's longstanding belief regarding Mary's conception: "We declare, pronounce, and define that the doctrine which holds that the most Blessed Virgin Mary, in the first instance of her conception, by a singular grace and privilege granted by Almighty God, in view of the merits of Jesus Christ, the Savior of the human race, was preserved free from all stain of original sin, is a doctrine revealed by God and therefore to be believed firmly and constantly by all the faithful."[1]

These words of *Ineffabilis Deus* echo throughout the parts of the Mass on December 8. The Opening Prayer, for example, recalls that the Father "preserved her from every stain by virtue of the Death of your Son, which you foresaw." In the Prayer over the Offerings, the Church professes her faith that Mary, on account of God's "prevenient grace," was "untouched by any stain of sin." Lastly, in the Prayer after Communion, we acknowledge that the Blessed Virgin "in a singular way" had been preserved from our common fault "in her Immaculate Conception."[2]

To appreciate more fully the dogma of Mary's Immaculate Conception, the Mass's first reading from the book of Genesis recounts the sin of our first parents. This account features a series of sins and accusations: Adam sins, he says to God, because of Eve, "the woman whom you gave to be with me" (Genesis 3:12). For her part, Eve blames her disobedience on the serpent who tricked her. The earth-bound serpent, alas, has no one else to pass on blame.

The eating of the forbidden fruit, however, is not in itself the core of Adam and Eve's sin. Rather, it was their disobedience to God's command. In this act, they manifested an unwillingness to listen to the loving, life-giving Logos spoken by the Father with the breath of the Spirit (see Genesis 1:1). To reject the Logos, or Word, is to reject life itself. To hear the Word with an open heart, on the other hand, is to give birth to the Word within one's heart and soul, and then to resound with that Word in the world. Many generations later, it was Mary of Nazareth who heard God speak in such a way that she would give birth to the Word.

At the end of the Genesis account, God says to the serpent (and, indirectly, to Eve): "I will put enmity between you and the woman, and between your seed and her seed; he shall bruise your head, and you shall bruise his heel" (Genesis 3:15). This *protoevangelium*—or "first announcement of the good news" following the "bad news" of the Fall—comes to fruition in the visit of the archangel Gabriel to the home of Mary, the subject of the Gospel reading for the Mass of the Immaculate Conception.

The Gospel passage begins: "The angel Gabriel was sent from God to a city of Galilee named Nazareth, to a virgin betrothed to a man whose name was Joseph, of the house of David; and the virgin's name was Mary. And he came to her and said, 'Hail, full of grace, the Lord is with you!'" (Luke 1:26–28). The salutation "full of grace" suggests the immaculate (i.e., sinless) state of Mary's soul.

Eve, our mother in the order of nature, said "no" to God's word, and death entered the world (see Romans 5:12–21, from the Office of Readings for the day). Mary, our mother in the order of grace, said "yes" to God's word, which ultimately brings eternal life through her Son. Herein lies the mystery of the Immaculate Conception. For Eve, who at her tempting had not yet experienced the effects of the Fall, succumbed to a lie. Mary, who was born without sin, nevertheless was not impervious to its effects; yet she gave herself entirely to the Word. How do we understand this mystery? It is rooted in the "singular grace" granted her at her conception. Mary worked with God's grace to respond in love to the message of an angel.

By the Immaculate Mary's "yes" to God, both heaven and earth are now more glorious than they had been in the beginning. Consider, for example, these extraordinary words of St. Anselm (c. 1033–1109), given in the Office of Readings:

> God is the Father of the created world and Mary the mother of the re-created world. God is the Father by whom all things were given life, and Mary the mother through whom all things were given new life. For God begot the Son, through whom all things were made, and Mary gave birth to him as the Savior of the world. Without God's Son, nothing could exist; without Mary's Son, nothing could be redeemed.

None of us can claim to be, like Mary, conceived immaculate. Yet each of us, like Mary, is called to be a "worthy dwelling" for the Son of God and, because of him, attain the joyful perfection of heaven. Mary is a perfect model, and so it is appropriate that we hold her Immaculate Conception among the most solemn of solemnities in the liturgical calendar.

The Immaculate Conception by Francisco de Zurbarán
(1628–1630) Museo Nacional del Prado, Madrid

The theology of the Immaculate Conception of the Blessed Virgin Mary remains so entrenched in modern Catholic culture that it is hard to imagine that theological arguments for and against this doctrine raged for centuries, not settled until a formal declaration by Pope Pius IX in 1854. Even without official approval, some Cistercian monasteries were known to celebrate liturgies honoring the Immaculate Conception by the twelfth century. Though different popes and councils issued theological statements and widened permissions, the question remained mired in controversy.

By the time he created this version of the Immaculate Conception, the Spanish painter Francisco de Zurbarán had just been appointed painter to King Philip IV. Known for his ascetic style and dramatic lighting, he gained acclaim in Seville, a city known as an "Immaculist" stronghold. Zurbarán had to face two challenges in depicting the Virgin. First, he had to illustrate "something that is not there—namely, original sin—directing our gaze to the absence of something invisible to the human eye."[3] Second, he had to navigate the difficult theological controversies and continuing debates around the subject, connecting the image to established Mariological conventions to keep it safely within theological limits.

Without any Gospel narratives illustrating the Immaculate Conception, Zurbarán turned to the "apocryphal woman," a biblical image of the Virgin found in the book of Revelation. The first verse of chapter twelve speaks of a great sign in the sky revealing a woman clothed with the sun, the moon under her feet, and crowned with twelve stars. Zurbarán painted accordingly, making the Virgin fill the sky, standing amidst sun-colored clouds and atop a crescent moon. The clouds part around her head to focus the viewer's attention on her face and starry halo, and a close look reveals that the reddish ring around her face is composed of the faces of child-like angels. Mary's innocence is indicated by her youthful appearance, while her downward glance and folded hands speak of her humility and prayerfulness, and her long hair falling upon her shoulders indicates her unmarried state (prior to her marriage to St. Joseph, that is). Importantly, Mary is shown without the child Jesus, indicating her condition before Christ's birth.

Floating in the clouds with the Virgin are symbols from the Old Testament, each referring to her purity, which later became customary honorific titles of the Virgin prayed in Marian litanies. In using these images, Zurbarán could refer to her immaculateness and perfection without overtly entering the thorny theological debate. On the right appears a looking glass, a reference to the spotless mirror mentioned in Wisdom 7:26, indicating that Mary perfectly reflects the glory of God without spot, just as the moon reflects the light of the sun. Above the mirror, a high stairway leads to a doorway, symbolizing the "stairway to heaven," a less common title for the Virgin today. In 2016, though, Pope Francis gave a homily calling Mary the "stairway God took to descend and draw near to us" and her immaculate womb the place where God "chose to mirror himself."[4]

On the top left appears a doorway, a reference to the *janua caeli*, or gate of heaven, taken directly from the Litany of Loretto. In a quite literal sense, Christ passed into the world through the "gate" of the Virgin's body. But a gate provides movement in two directions, and in poetic terms, Mary can be seen not only as the portal of heaven to earth, but also earth to heaven, as the pious phrase "to Jesus through Mary" rightly indicates. Accordingly, many saints and popes have described devotion to the Blessed Mother as the surest and safest path to Christ and thereby heaven itself.

Lastly, a circular columned building appears on the left, a reference to Mary as temple of the Holy Spirit, a title once common in litanies of the Virgin but which no longer appears. Just as God chose to dwell in the Temple of Jerusalem, at the Incarnation, God chose to dwell in the womb of the Virgin by being overshadowed by the Holy Spirit. Moreover, it is said that Mary's immaculateness was itself a fruit of the Holy Spirit's work in preparing her, and so not only did her womb contain Christ, but God's own glory in the Holy Spirit.

As the theology of the Immaculate Conception developed and was declared a dogma by the Church, the secondary symbols of the Virgin's litany began to disappear, and her prayerful pose alone in the sky began to speak for itself. But Zurbarán's painting reminds us today of her role in salvation, entirely dependent on the virtues and salvific action of her Son, and therefore the Father and the Spirit. Mary is not a goddess, but a woman given the special privilege of receiving a foretaste of the spotless perfection promised to all Christians. In that way, she gives humanity hope that what God accomplished in her will be accomplished in all who love him.

* * * * * *

Celebrating the
Immaculate Conception

A Patronal Feast

This solemnity marks the feast day of the patroness of the United States, as well as Brazil, Spain, the Philippines, and Korea. After the US bishops chose the patronage of "the Virgin Mary, conceived without Sin," this was confirmed by Pope Pius IX in 1847, seven years before the Immaculate Conception was proclaimed a dogma in 1854. In many Catholic countries, this solemnity is a public holiday. Some traditions include honoring one's mother and grandmothers on the Immaculate Conception, such as in Panama, where it is celebrated as Mother's Day.

Marian Processions

In Manila, Philippines, this feast day is marked with a grand procession in honor of Our Lady, in which a variety of statues and images are carried, representing nearly a hundred different titles of Mary. The various figures of Mary are carried on *carrozas*, carriages decorated with flowers. The procession is accompanied by a brass band and ceremoniously makes its way through the old city to the cathedral, which is dedicated to the Immaculate Conception. In 2017, the Immaculate Conception was declared a national holiday in the Philippines.

In parts of Spain, this patronal feast is celebrated with the same fervor as the feast of Corpus Christi. In one of his letters, W. B. Yeats mentions the festivities in Seville, noting a special kind of dance for this day known as *los Seises*: "In a few days, we motor to Seville, where on the Feast of the Immaculate Conception I shall see the sixteen boys dance in front of the high altar."[5] This "Dance of the Sixes" is a unique tradition dating back more than five hundred years, featuring choir boys performing a short dance before the celebration of Mass.

Marian processions take place in many parish churches and Catholic schools around the world. Children take part in presenting flowers to the Blessed Mother, raised on a *bier* (the name for the traditional platform for carrying a statue in procession). In some processions, an image or statue of Mary is surrounded by candlelight as the Litany of Loreto is prayed, which features all of her wonderful titles. In the home, a beautiful practice is to incorporate a simple procession of flowers to Mary as a part of the conclusion of the Novena.

Novena of the Immaculate Conception

During the days preceding and ending on this feast, there is a popular tradition of praying a novena. This is prayed once each day for nine days, its name taken from the Latin word *novem* (the number nine). The *Directory on Popular Piety* describes the novena of the Immaculate Conception: "There can be no doubt that the feast of the pure and sinless Conception of the Virgin Mary, which is a fundamental preparation for the Lord's coming into the world, harmonizes perfectly with many of the salient themes of Advent."[6] This novena embarks on a scriptural journey with Mary to begin the Advent season, highlighting biblical texts from Genesis 3:15, and ending with the salutation of the angel Gabriel to the one who is "full of grace" (see Luke 1:31–33).

Your Praises We Sing

The musical treasury of the Church contains a great multitude of compositions written in Our Lady's honor, including several hymns we know and love, such as "Immaculate Mary," "Sing of Mary, Pure and Lowly," and the many settings of the Ave Maria. Every Catholic should know a verse of at least one Marian hymn by heart. The traditional Marian antiphon that begins in the Advent season is the *Alma redemptoris mater*. Listen to a recording online and learn to sing the Marian antiphons that correspond to each season. This is a song that we share universally in the Western church. It is usually sung at the conclusion of Compline (Night Prayer).

Sacred Symbols

On solemnities, we celebrate in song and with many other symbols of festivity. For the celebration of Mass in parishes, flowers can be used around the altar on the Immaculate Conception, though they are not typically seen during the Advent season. Just as the domestic church mirrors the universal church, liturgical symbols incorporated into the home serve as a reminder of extraordinary celebrations: lilies and roses are particular signs of Mary's purity in honor of this extraordinary mystery.

In his great opus *The Liturgical Year*, Dom Prosper Guéranger describes the story of the celebration on this feast day after it was solemnly proclaimed by Pope Pius IX in 1854. In recognition of their defense of the belief in Mary's Immaculate Conception over the centuries, members of the Franciscan order were invited to Rome for the celebration. There, they presented a beautiful pair of symbols. When the pope had crowned the statue of Our Lady with a "splendid diadem," the Franciscans offered the Pope branches of silver lilies and silver roses. "The lilies and the roses were symbolical of Mary's purity and love; the whiteness of the silver was the emblem of the lovely brightness of that orb, on which is reflected the light of the Sun; for, as the Canticle says of Mary, 'she is beautiful as the moon.'"[7]

The Nativity of the Lord
(Christmas)

December 25

The celebration of Christmas has generated many songs, movies, foods, and other traditions. Perhaps more importantly, it has also fostered numerous cultural stories, each of which, to a greater or lesser degree, helps illustrate the meaning of the season. Clement Moore's "A Visit from St. Nicholas" (popularly known as "'Twas the night before Christmas") tells in verse of a father's nighttime run-in with the gift-giving St. Nicholas. The story of "The Nutcracker and the Mouse King," by E. T. A. Hoffmann, has been told and retold in words, ballets, and cartoons. And Charles Dickens' *A Christmas Carol* has made the villain-turned-hero "Scrooge" a common name.

These stories are deeply engrained in how the Western world understands and celebrates Christmas, and they remain favorites even in today's secular society. But there is one other book that gets more directly to the heart of the matter at this time of year. Though it predates the above-mentioned popular stories by centuries, it is not as well-known. This little book with a big message is entitled *On the Incarnation*, written by St. Athanasius of Alexandria around the year 319. As its title suggests, this work treats the Incarnation of the Word, and it seeks to answer one of the most fundamental questions of our Faith: Why did God become man?

Spoiler alert, in case you are tempted to read St. Athanasius' book: God became man so that man might become God. While reindeer, nutcrackers, and ghosts of Christmas past, present, and future may live on the surface of the Christmas season, the heart of the Christmas mystery is that by taking on our nature, God allows us to share in his nature.

The celebration of Christmas is so significant that the Church offers four different Mass settings for the solemnity: Vigil Mass, Mass during the Night, Mass at Dawn, and Mass during the Day. It is as if four different sets of readings and prayers are necessary to capture the significance of the Word taking on human flesh. The Gospel reading for the Vigil Mass, for example, recounts the genealogy of Jesus and the appearance of the angel to St. Joseph. For Mass during the Night, the Church recounts the visit of the heavenly host to the shepherds, whereas the reading for Mass at Dawn tells the story of the shepherds meeting Jesus, Mary, and Joseph at the manger. Finally, for Mass during the Day, we hear not a story as such but the lyrical prologue of St. John's Gospel, which encapsulates the story of Christmas in theological terms: "In the beginning was the Word, and the Word was with God, and the Word was God … And the Word became flesh and dwelt among us" (John 1:1, 14).

Whether it is the vivid, heart-warming stories of the angels, the shepherds, and the manger, or the more theologically conceptual account from St. John, the Christmas narrative reveals the most serious of truths: God comes to save us from sin and death and, even more, make us partakers in his own divine nature.

In the Office of Readings for the Day, St. Leo the Great (c. 400–461) presents the central meaning of Christmas, as St. Athanasius had done before him: "Dearly beloved, today our Savior is born; let us rejoice. Sadness should have no place on the birthday of life. The fear of death has been swallowed up; life brings us joy with the promise of eternal happiness … In the fullness of time … the Son of God took for himself our common humanity in order to reconcile it with its creator. He came to overthrow the devil, the origin of death, in that very nature by which [the devil] had overthrown mankind." The gifts of Santa Claus, then, are mere tokens of the greatest gift given us at Christmas—the gift of new life.

Consider how this great gift exchange—our humanity for Christ's divinity—appears throughout the prayers of the various Masses on Christmas. In the Opening Prayer for Mass during Christmas Day, the priest prays: "O God, who wonderfully created the dignity of human nature and still more wonderfully restored it, grant, we pray, that we may share in the divinity of Christ, who humbled himself to share in our humanity." In the Prayer over the Offerings at the Mass during the Night, he says: "May the oblation of this day's feast be pleasing to you, O Lord, we pray, that through this most holy exchange we may be found in the likeness of Christ, in whom our nature is united to you." And during one of the possible prefaces at Christmas Masses (prayed immediately before the *Sanctus*), the celebrant prays in the people's name that through the birth of Christ "the holy exchange that restores our life has shone forth today in splendor: when our frailty is assumed by your Word not only does human mortality receive unending honor but by this wondrous union we, too, are made eternal."

This "divinization," as it is called, is essentially a new creation, one even better than the original creation. At that creation, Father, Son, and Spirit (see Genesis 1:1) made Adam in the "image and likeness" of God (see Genesis 1:26–27). But "seduced by the devil, [Adam] wanted to 'be like God,' but 'without God, before God, and not in accordance with God'" (CCC 398). With the birth of Jesus comes the dawn of God's new creation. Here is born the new Adam, described in the second reading for Mass during Christmas Day as the Son "through whom also he created the ages. He reflects the glory of God and bears the very stamp of his nature" (Hebrews 1:2–3). This Adam—the Word of the Father spoken in the Holy Spirit—lifts fallen man to unimaginable heights.

The Solemnity of the Nativity of the Lord celebrates a mystery so much grander than passing gifts and earthly sentiments. It celebrates an exchange of gifts between heaven and earth: At the birth of Jesus, God becomes one of us so that we can abide eternally within the heart of God himself.

The Mystic Nativity by Sandro Botticelli
(1500) National Gallery, London

The birth of Christ shatters many expectations. Far from the mere silent night of sentimental greeting cards, it marks the moment when "infinity dwindled to infancy," as the Jesuit poet Gerard Manley Hopkins puts it. The eternal God who exists beyond space and time did not come as a powerful avenging warrior but as a helpless child born in a feeding trough. The birth of Jesus fulfills the long-prophesied coming of *Immanuel*, the Hebrew name meaning "God with us." Herein lies the challenge for an artist portraying the Nativity: How to show the infinite magnitude of Christ's birth as an event of eternal significance yet wrapped in hidden modesty. Sandro Botticelli's *Mystical Nativity*, however, leaves no room for ambiguity. Though Christ is born a helpless baby laid next to cattle and donkeys, the sky opens and angels rejoice, marking that God-with-us is not only a person, but a new relationship between finite and infinite, time and eternity, heaven and earth.

Botticelli, a Florentine painter of the early Renaissance, created many large altar pieces, historical scenes, and mythological depictions, and he was later called to Rome to complete three murals in the Sistine Chapel. The *Mystical Nativity*, however, is only thirty inches wide and is his only signed work, causing some historians to see it as an intensely personal piece. In common Renaissance practice, he gave the painting a geometric underpinning, dividing it into three horizontal layers centered on the child Christ, St. Joseph, and the Blessed Virgin Mary. Though kneeling, Mary's body appears like a column, marking the center of the painting. Together with the long neck of the donkey, her gaze of adoration points to the infant Jesus, who lies naked and reaches up to embrace her. St. Joseph sleeps to his left, a traditional indicator of his chastity and, therefore, of the Virgin's purity. At the left, angels lead the three Magi to see the child, while on the right, they lead shepherds, signifying that Christ's salvation is for the powerful and the poor alike. In a similar vein, the ox was considered a "clean" or lawful animal in Judaism, while the donkey was not, so the appearance of both indicates that Christ has come for both Jews and Gentiles.

In Botticelli's rendering, the traditional stable is both a cave and a wooden structure, a common practice in the Holy Land, where animals were housed in natural hollows with fenced pens in front. But the cave itself carries deep theological significance. Like water, which is necessary for life yet can bring the destruction of a flood, a cave provides a hidden place of safety from threat, yet is closely associated with darkness, death, and even the underworld of hell. So in his redemptive mission, Christ is born precisely into the darkness of the fallen human condition, with the earthly cave—including his naked body laid on a sheet—prefiguring his three days in the tomb and his descent into the realm of the dead. Meanwhile, the stable's two posts retain the appearance of trees, recalling both the tree of Eden which led to humanity's fall and the redemptive tree of the Cross. It also symbolically prefigures Christ's vocation of carpenter, one who has authority over trees and lumber—the material of his future cross—and likewise over both sin and redemption.

Importantly, the simple narrative of the Holy Family is framed above and below by rejoicing angels, beings normally hidden from human view. The crown of angels above indicates the interconnectedness of heaven and earth, opening a golden portal through which Christ enters humanity's condition to lead it back to the Father. Each of the angels carries an olive branch, a symbol of peace between God and man since the time of Noah when the dove brought an olive leaf back to the ark, indicating the end of the great Flood. Botticelli thereby reveals that God has become man so that man might share in his divinity, and the definitive restoration of peace has begun.

The angels also honor the Virgin, since the ribbons which flutter from the branches bear inscriptions revealing the twelve "privileges" given to the Virgin, coming from a prayer preached by Girolamo Savonarola after a mystical vision.[8] Honorific titles particular to the Nativity fittingly appear, including *Spouse of the Father*, *Mother of God*, *Singular Tabernacle of the Holy Spirit*, *Virgin of Virgins*, and *Queen Honored Above All Creatures*, each followed by the request that she intercede for those who honor her. Together these honorific names form a "crown" of prayer offered by the faithful, and so delicate crowns indicating her queenship hang below the ribbons. The three colors of the angels' garments likewise arise from the preacher's vision, in which he saw the Virgin's crown bedecked with gems—green jasper, white pearls, and red carbuncles.

At the bottom of the painting, three angels, again dressed in red, white, and green, embrace and kiss three human beings, with the angel in the left pair holding a ribbon inscribed with the angelic salutation to the shepherds: "peace on earth to men of good will." While various interpretations of this unusual scene abound, the figures likely refer to Psalm 85, which speaks of God's plan of salvation for the world, which seems to summarize the entire painting: "Mercy and faithfulness will meet; righteousness and peace will kiss each other. Faithfulness will spring up from the ground, and righteousness will look down from heaven" (Psalm 85:10–11). In other words, God's eternal love meets those who believe in Christ, and the righteousness of God's justice, which once brought fear, now brings peace. Christ's humanity, which comes from the "ground" like the dust of which Adam was made, now meets the perfection of Christ's divinity, which comes from heaven. Here lies the essence of the Nativity, far beyond cute babies and maternal tenderness. God comes to earth in self-giving love, becoming human so that humans might become divine, and becoming weak so that all of creation might grow strong.

Celebrating Christmas

Of all the solemnities of the year, Christmas is the one we most often think of when we look to traditions in the home. Stores are filled with Christian symbols waiting to be bought and used to decorate the domestic Church. This is a great opportunity to delve more deeply into the meaning of this time, and to incorporate this rich symbolism more fully into our family traditions.

The Manger Scene or *Crèche*

The Christmas manger scene, also known as *crèche* or *praesepio,* is a custom observed in churches and homes throughout the world. From the larger-than-life figures erected in St. Peter's Square in Rome to tiny figures in a child's room, the nativity scene is often set up with a wooden shed containing a crib to hold the newborn King. Traditionally, the infant Jesus is kept hidden during the days leading up to Christmas, and then ceremoniously placed in the manger following Midnight Mass.

The *crèche* is a shrine to our Lord, surrounded by Mary, Joseph, shepherds, and the animals that witnessed the Nativity. Though they are not mentioned in Luke's Gospel, the image of the ox and the donkey around the manger is foretold in Isaiah 1:3—"The ox knows its owner, and the donkey its master's crib." Here we see the humility of the mystery of the Incarnation—even unintelligent animals witness the Lord's coming in the lowliness of a babe in a manger. There is a beautiful traditional Christmas responsory from the traditional office of Matins that expresses this great mystery:

> *O magnum mysterium,*
> *et admirabile sacramentum,*
> *ut animalia viderent Dominum natum,*
> *iacentem in praesepio!*
> *Beata Virgo, cujus viscera*
> *meruerunt portare*
> *Dominum Iesum Christum.*
> *Alleluia!*

> O great mystery,
> and wonderful sacrament,
> that animals should see the newborn Lord,
> lying in a manger!
> Blessed is the virgin whose womb
> was worthy to bear
> the Lord, Jesus Christ.
> Alleluia!

Blessing of the Christmas Tree

While stores start setting up Christmas trees in October, the Catholic custom of blessing the Christmas tree happens just before Christmas. One story from the eighth century describes St. Boniface coming upon a group of pagans worshipping an oak tree. To prevent them from worshipping false gods (in this case, the pagan god Thor), Boniface cut down the tree. Since he was not struck down by lightning, as they expected, he converted them on the spot. The legend continues that a fir tree grew out of the fallen oak, or that Boniface planted one in the same place. This became a Christian

symbol of new life in Christ. This brings to mind the Cross, made of wood, as the Tree of Life.

In the book *Catholic Household Blessings and Prayers,* there is a blessing of a Christmas tree for home use. One of the intercessions during the blessing asks, "[May] this tree of lights remind us of the tree of glory on which Christ accomplished our salvation."[9] This blessing service can be prayed before the evening meal, and includes readings, intercessions, and suitable carols. It concludes with the following words: "Lord God, let your blessing come upon us as we illumine this tree. May the light and cheer it gives be a sign of the joy that fills our hearts. May all who delight in this tree come to the knowledge and joy of salvation. We ask this through Christ our Lord. Amen."[10]

After the blessing is prayed, the lights that adorn the Christmas tree are lit for the first time. The longstanding custom is to keep the tree up until the feast of the Presentation of the Lord on February 2.

Decorating and Feasting

Holly, mistletoe, yule logs, and pudding are all Christmas traditions that have secular origins but quickly became a part of the Christian celebration of the Nativity of the Lord. Both St. Augustine of Canterbury and St. Gregory the Great sanctioned the "Christianizing" of older festive traditions, offering them now to these outward pleasures of joy and merriment.[11] One can taste twelve puddings, one on each of the twelve days following Christmas (i.e., Christmas to Epiphany), made by friends or neighbors. An English tradition uses cakes of different varieties, depending on the region, bringing luck for the coming year.

A Carol to Sing

"What sweeter music can we bring than a carol for to sing the birth of this our heavenly King?"[12] Aside from decorating and feasting as staples of the domestic church during the Christmas season, another popular activity is caroling. While it is no longer common in most areas to go door-to-door singing carols to one's neighbors, many families retain the tradition of singing or listening to carols in the home. In addition, many parishes sing carols before Christmas Masses.

One tradition popularized in English churches and colleges has been brought into the sphere of Catholic devotional services: the Festival of Lessons and Carols. The service follows a series of nine Scripture passages, from the story of Creation and the Fall to the prophecies of the Incarnation. It is interspersed with carols and prayers to reflect on the readings. The final passage is normally taken from the prologue of John's Gospel: "In the beginning was the Word, and the Word was with God, and the Word was God … And the Word became flesh and made his dwelling among us, and we saw his glory, the glory as of the Father's only Son, full of grace and truth" (John 1:1, 14).

Mary, the Holy Mother of God

January 1

Some ancient philosophies emphasize the transcendent realm over the earthly. Plato, for example, held that the things we see in the present world are merely shadows and images of true things that exist in a world beyond us. Similarly, some religions downplay the material world in favor of the spiritual, either because the material world is considered an illusion or evil. In such a religion, redemption consists of escaping the world of the senses for the "purer," true spiritual world.

The Catholic Faith is not such a religion, as the Solemnity of Mary, the Holy Mother of God makes clear. Catholics see the world as a marriage of the spiritual and material, not a divorce of these two realties. The very title of Mary as "Mother of God" shows the intrinsic connection between the material and spiritual realms. Let's consider what this means. First, notice that the Second Person of the Trinity—eternal, infinite, omnipotent—becomes incarnate through a human mother! Second, "Mother of God" means that humanity and divinity, the material and the spiritual, earth and heaven, exist inseparably from the point of the incarnation of Jesus in the womb of Mary, his human mother.

This solemnity has had other names in the Church's history, all of which likewise emphasize the earthiness of this fundamental tenet of the faith. The Roman Missal still refers to this day as "The Octave Day of the Nativity of the Lord." Aside from Easter, Christmas is the foremost mystery of our Faith. Since the celebration of the Resurrection on Easter cannot be contained within a twenty-four-hour period (which is why we celebrate it for eight days during the Octave of Easter, as well as every Sunday), the celebration of Christmas lasts eight days. The meaning of this solemnity, then, is the same as that of Christmas: "The Word became flesh, and we have seen his glory." In Jesus, our faith in God is tangible; it is no longer abstract.

Another of this day's traditional titles, "The Circumcision of Our Lord," similarly expresses the human dimension of our faith. The Gospel reading on this day recounts the visit of the shepherds to the Holy Family after the birth of Jesus, the same story that the Church recounts at Christmas Mass at Dawn. But today, the Church concludes the reading with this extra detail: "And at the end of eight days, when he was circumcised, he was called Jesus, the name given by the angel before he was conceived in the womb" (Luke 2:21). From the time of Abraham, every male child was circumcised on the eighth day as a sign of being a part of the covenant with God (see Genesis 17:9–14). The Lord now has a mother, a body, a human name, and—as signaled by his circumcision—physical pain. This first day of the civic calendar announces through the circumcision of Jesus that he is among us, one of us, suffering with us, and beginning the year with us.

Still another connection between our eternal, supernatural religion and our temporal, mundane life is that this solemnity coincides with the first day of the secular year. This first day of the year had been celebrated in Rome prior to Christ's coming. Janus, the two-faced Roman god of beginnings and endings, is where the name "January" for the first month of the year is derived. With the coming of Jesus—the Alpha and Omega, the beginning and the end of all time—Janus finds his true bearings. Though the texts and prayers of this day's liturgies do not acknowledge the start of the civil year (the Church, after all, has already begun its new liturgical year with the start of Advent some weeks before), marking its first day helps the Church on earth to thank God for blessings received over the past year and ask for his ongoing care in the year ahead.

But none of these human dimensions of our faith that this day expresses—its connection to Christmas, to Jesus' human body, to his entering into time itself—would have been possible without Mary agreeing to become the Mother of God. It is thus this dimension of the day that rises to the top.

After all, the very face of Jesus comes from his mother Mary. Indeed, he would have physically resembled her to some extent—he may have had her eyes, her expressions, her smile. Through this face, God now speaks: "In the past God spoke to our ancestors through the prophets; in these last days, he has spoken to us through the Son" (verse for the Gospel acclamation). We read in the Old Testament about how God's people, when they heard the thunderous voice of the Lord, were afraid and sent Moses to hear God in their stead (see Exodus 20:18–19; and Deuteronomy 5:22–28; 18:16–18). At the Incarnation, the same God speaks in a different way, a human way, through Jesus' voice and face, given him by the holy Mother of God, Mary.

And it is with this body—one like yours and mine—that this same voice can praise and adore the Father in our name and can offer his body and soul to him. As St. Athanasius explains in the Office of Readings for this day, the Word "had to be like his brothers in all things. He had then to take a body like ours. This explains the fact of Mary's presence: she is to provide him with a body of his own, to be offered for our sake … What was born of Mary was therefore human by nature … and the body of the Lord was a true body: It was a true body because it was the same as ours."

January 1, the Solemnity of Mary, the Holy Mother of God, proclaims the accessibility of our Catholic Faith—it is human, incarnate, tangible—even as it calls us to the higher things—divinity, heaven, and glory—in the new year.

Madonna in the Church by Jan Van Eyck
(1428) Gemäldegalerie, State Museum, Berlin

J an Van Eyck's fifteenth-century *Madonna in the Church* is aptly named—the Blessed Virgin stands in a Gothic cathedral rendered with astonishingly detailed realism. As the court painter to the king of Holland, Van Eyck was renowned in his own day for his virtuosity in precisely rendering details such as clothing, carpets, jewels, faces, landscapes, and architecture. And this tiny painting, a mere twelve inches high, is no exception, as he even includes cobwebs hanging from the ceiling near the windows. Yet within this otherwise believable church stands a Virgin of tremendous proportions, who would be nearly sixty feet tall if the painting were meant to be literal. But literal, it is not. Instead, it shows Van Eyck's masterful combination of realism and symbolism, revealing the Virgin Mary as not only tender Mother, but also as the powerful Queen of Heaven and image of the Church. More importantly, she is not only the mother of Jesus, but the Mother of *God*.

At first glance, this image seems simple, with the Virgin and Child standing peacefully in an empty church. But Van Eyck masterfully includes minute detail and theological symbolism to give it layers of meaning. First, the Virgin and Christ stand in a church because Mary is seen as a "type" of the Church itself. In Scripture studies, typology is the study of symbols that prefigure God's plan of salvation and prepare humanity for its fulfillment. Adam, the first man, is seen as a type of Christ, the New Man, who brings salvation to the world damaged by Adam's sin. Similarly, Mary is seen as the New Eve. But the Virgin was also the "place" where Christ dwelled on earth as his body was formed in her womb. The church building, then, is now the new place where Christ's Mystical Body assembles and takes shape. Placing Christ and the Virgin in a church recalls and amplifies this reality.

In a second layer of symbolism, the use of light becomes an important theological marker for Van Eyck. As one of the earliest masters of the use of oil paints, he was able to put down layers of color over clear glazes, giving the image a luminous glow not possible with earlier tempera paints, which laid down only flat areas of color. Scholars have analyzed the many meanings of the use of light in the image, most notably that which floods in the high windows and forms two pools on the floor. In one sense, the lighting is natural and expected and the architecture completely accurate. Light floods in from above, in sharp contrast to the dark regions below. Already this forms an analogy with the light of heaven illuminating this fallen world. Since churches were traditionally built facing east, the left side of the painting would face north, which would never have the natural lighting of a south wall. Van Eyck subtly implies that the light here

must be *supernatural* light, which seems familiar yet comes from beyond the natural realm.

Light has other meanings as well. In medieval theology, light is seen as more than illumination for the eye but as an attribute of God that makes things knowable, thus revealing their inner meaning to the mind. Christ, of course, is the Light of the World because he makes the Father knowable to humanity, and Mary was the bearer of this light to the world. Since the Church has given Mary the title *Mother of God*—rather than "mother of Jesus' humanity"— the conception of Jesus is sometimes portrayed as being made possible by divine light. A homily of St. Bernard of Clairvaux compares Jesus' conception and birth to the brilliant light of the sun passing through a prism. So Van Eyck takes the natural symbolism of the window and makes it a sign of the miraculous conception of Christ, the God–Man.

The painting contains numerous other tiny details which again reinforce the fundamental Catholic notion of sacramentality: the invisible God is known through matter as revealed in human history. Directly over Mary's left shoulder, a small shrine appears in the church, showing a wooden statue of the Virgin and Child lit by two candles. In normal space and time, the faithful encounter and honor Mary through a sacred image. But now she stands outside of space and time in the great nave of the church. Moreover, the pointed-arched woodwork in the back of the church contains small carved scenes involving praise of the Virgin. The first illustrates the Annunciation to Mary of Jesus' conception by the archangel Gabriel, who calls her full of grace. The second shows her coronation as Queen of Heaven, receiving the highest possible praise from Christ himself. To these real-looking carvings are added a pair of "real" angels visible through the screen in the cathedral sanctuary, singing her praises from large choir books. Here again, the tangibility of realism—carved statues—meets the breaking in of heavenly beings.

Van Eyck's little image partakes of the large claim of the Catholic Faith: When the immaterial God took on flesh, he made it possible for material things to rise to heavenly perfection, even while still in this world. Bread becomes Christ's Body, and wine becomes his Blood. Water washes the soul in the sacrament of Baptism, and oil brings strength and healing in the Anointing of the Sick. So, too, *Madonna in the Church* shows how a statue of the Virgin and Child mediates the reality of their heavenly presence. As in all Marian theology, everything true about Mary speaks of the reality of Christ. She is image of the Church and Mother of God precisely because she bore Christ the God–Man, who makes his divine life available to the world with a child-like tenderness, revealing the love of the Father for all that he has made.

Celebrating the Solemnity of Mary, the Holy Mother of God

This is the day on which we celebrate above all the motherhood of Mary, the *Theotokos* (God-bearer).[13] This title tells us more about Jesus than about Mary, as it indicates his human and divine natures. God chose Mary to be the mother of the Son, and with her *fiat* she became the Mother of God, given in turn to us as our spiritual mother.

The Mystery of Time

Eight days after Jesus' birth, we celebrate this feast in honor of the Motherhood of Mary. In liturgical time, an octave (eight days) is a way of extending the joyful celebration of a great feast, the number eight symbolizing eternity, that great heavenly "day" without end. In the Roman rite of the Church, the other feast that is celebrated as an octave is Easter.

On this day, we also celebrate the start of the civil new year. These two celebrations are not at odds with one another; rather, they are apt reminders to us of the mystery of time. As we contemplate the work of God in salvation history, through the birth of Christ and the maternity of Mary, we can also contemplate the moments of the divine interacting in our own lives.

Popular Traditions

There are many secular traditions associated with the civil new year, such as making resolutions or seeking "good luck." For instance, in some Eastern European cultures, a mixture of wheat and honey is thrown on the ceiling to see how much will stick, which indicates the family's fortune in the coming year. In the context of the Faith, there are several traditions that help us to keep the day in light of the Christian mysteries.

Many parishes incorporate a time of prolonged Eucharistic adoration concluding with benediction and Mass on the evening of December 31. It is important to see adoration on this evening in context of the mystery of God in time, especially during the Christmas season. Here, we are not so much marking the passing of time but offering the new year to the Lord, as all time belongs to him. This recalls the words from the blessing of the Paschal candle at the Easter Vigil: "Christ yesterday and today, the Beginning and the End, the Alpha and the Omega. All time belongs to him and all the ages. To him be glory and power through every age and for ever. Amen."[14]

Singing in the New Year

One of the popular pious exercises on the evening of December 31 is the public singing of the hymn *Te Deum*, which you may hear if you attend Mass or Eucharistic adoration on this evening. This prayer is a great proclamation of public rejoicing, singing, "We praise thee, O God!" The Church affirms this practice on this day in particular "as an act of community praise and thanksgiving to God for the graces received from Him as the year draws to a close."[15]

To complement the *Te Deum*, the hymn *Veni Creator Spiritus* (Come, Creator Spirit) is sung on January 1. This ninth-century Latin hymn is attributed to the monk Rabanus Maurus, and it implores the help of the Holy Spirit. The Church encourages the practice of singing this hymn on this day so "the faithful can pray that the Spirit may direct their thoughts and actions, and those of the community during the course of the year."[16] Sing in the New Year with these two great hymns, either at Mass in your parish or in your home.

Prayer for Peace

On this solemnity, an additional prayer intention for us to keep in mind is peace in our world. The Church keeps this prayer close, observing the World Day of Peace established in 1967. Today, the Church's prayer is focused on the sacredness of life, the dignity of the human person, solidarity and fraternity, and peace in the world. This prayer is particularly fitting as we rejoice in this season at the coming of the Messiah, the Prince of Peace.

A Mary-Centered Year

It is easy to get swept up in secular practices of celebrating the beginning of the new year. Framed in the context of the mystery of time, the Christian family can keep this day holy. On this day dedicated to the Mother of God and our mother, focus on how Marian devotion can support your family's domestic Church throughout the year. This is a good day to plan Marian consecrations and make a renewed commitment to Marian devotion. Mary is honored above all because she brings us to Christ. Through her *fiat* and her example, she is a model of holiness for all of us, and so leads us to her Son. One popular practice on all Marian feast days is to recite the Litany of Loreto, especially after praying the Rosary. This Litany comes from the Middle Ages and lists the titles and invocations of Mary. These highlight her virtues, privileges, and example for us all.

The Epiphany of the Lord

January 6

The third and final solemnity of the Christmas Season celebrates the Epiphany of the Lord. Like the solemnities of Christmas and Mary, Mother of God, the Epiphany brings before us the mystery of the Incarnation: God takes on flesh through a human mother. Unlike the season's first two solemnities, however, the Epiphany reveals the grander mystery in the mind of God.

In the second reading for Mass, St. Paul tells us that "the mystery was made known to me by revelation" (Ephesians 3:3). What is the "mystery" to which Paul refers? Here, "mystery" is not a reference to the seemingly impenetrable truths of faith, such as God is three and one; Jesus is God and man; Mary is both virgin and mother. While these truths are mysteries of the faith, the Christian mystery that St. Paul writes of here is God's plan for the creation and redemption of the world through Christ.

The celebration of Epiphany manifests this plan, for it recalls how a seemingly insignificant baby, born to unknown parents in a cave in a Roman outpost, was to rule—and save—the entire world. The liturgy today illuminates this divine mystery through its themes of light, its call to the Gentiles, and its connection with Jesus' power and divinity.

First, light pervades significant portions of the Epiphany texts, particularly in the first reading of the Mass from the prophet Isaiah (which is also used as the first reading in the solemnity's Office of Readings): "Arise, shine; for your light has come, and the glory of the LORD has risen upon you. For behold, darkness shall cover the earth, and thick darkness the peoples; but the LORD will arise upon you, and his glory will be seen upon you. And nations shall walk by your light, and kings in the brightness of your rising" (Isaiah 60:1–3). One luminous character of the day's reading is the star. The wise men relate in the Gospel of Matthew how they "saw his star at its rising and have come to do him homage" (Matthew 2:2; used for the Gospel acclamation for this solemnity). In a commentary on this passage, St. Peter Chrysologus identifies the star with Jesus himself: "Today the Magi find, crying in a manger, the one they have followed as he shone in the sky … the one they have long awaited as he lay hidden among the stars." Jesus is called the "Morning Star" in the Easter *Exsultet*, and Mary shines as "Star of the Sea" in the Night Prayer hymn *Ave, Maris Stella*. Stars thus play an important part in the "plan of the mystery."

The inclusion of the Gentiles is a second aspect of this solemnity that announces the universal character of God's plan of salvation. The coming of Jesus is not merely for the Jewish children of Abraham but for all on earth. As the entrance antiphon for the Vigil Mass says, "Arise, Jerusalem, and look to the East and see your children gathered from the rising to the setting of the sun." The responsorial psalm likewise announces the universality of God's design: "Lord, every nation on earth will adore you" (see Psalm 72:11). The "magi from the east" of the Gospel reading embody the plan of salvation that has spilled over beyond the borders of Israel. As St. Paul summarizes, "The Gentiles are fellow heirs, members of the same body, and partakers of the promise in Christ Jesus through the gospel" (Ephesians 3:6).

Apart from the biblical texts chosen by the Church for this solemnity, the Church also uses a church building to make this universal point. In Rome, the tradition of "stational" churches sees the pope celebrate particular Masses at specific churches, or "stations," throughout the city on specific days of the liturgical year. On this solemnity celebrating the Lord's mission to save all peoples, the stational church is St. Peter's Basilica, which is a monument to the nations, standing with open arms to the world's inhabitants from East to West.

Third, Epiphany's connections to other celebrations that show Christ revealing the divine glory also serve as markers for God's plan for the world's redemption. In fact, the antiphon for the Canticle of Mary at evening prayer on the day of Epiphany proclaims: "Three mysteries mark this holy day: today the star leads the Magi to the infant Christ; today water is changed into wine for the wedding feast; today Christ wills to be baptized by John in the river Jordan to bring us salvation." The appearance of the star, as we have seen, is an obvious mystery marking the day. But the other two events—Jesus changing water into wine at the wedding feast of Cana and his baptism by John in the Jordan—may seem out of place. Why are these two events recalled on the Solemnity of the Epiphany? Because they both show God's power manifesting itself in human history. These various epiphanies demonstrate the "plan of the mystery" that the Father seeks to make known to the world.

In Jesus' time, of course, many could (or would) not see beneath the surface to the great saving mystery that he embodied. Today, too, many are unable to peer into the mind and heart of God made manifest through his Church and her Liturgy. Perhaps the Prayer after Communion for the Epiphany Mass during the Day should continue to ring in our ears throughout the year: "Go before us with heavenly light, O Lord, always and everywhere, that we may perceive with clear sight and revere with true affection the mystery in which you have willed us to participate."

Adoration of the Magi by Domenico Ghirlandaio
(1488) Oespedale degli Innocenti, Florence

The word "epiphany" comes from the Greek term *phainein*, meaning "to show" or "to shine." In the story of the three Magi (see Matthew 2:1–12), epiphany has a double meaning: God shows his love for the world by becoming incarnate as an infant, and he reveals his power to conquer sin and death by showing his kingship over heaven and earth. In his *Adoration of the Magi*, Domenico Ghirlandaio captures this duality in an exuberant fashion. Though the artist portrays Jesus as surrounded by an ox and a donkey in a stable, he nonetheless reigns from the throne of his mother's lap to be adored by kings below and praised by singing angels above. Here, heaven and earth meet. So while the nativity of Jesus is a historical event, Ghirlandaio's version prefigures the glory of heaven to come—and was rendered for a specific audience: parentless children and those who cared for them.

Ghirlandaio's commission for the *Adoration* came from Florence's Oespedale degli Innocenti, the Hospital of the Innocents, a home for abandoned children funded by the city's guild of silk merchants. Fittingly, it took its name not only from the innocent children who came to its doors, but also from the account of the massacre of the innocents in Mathew's Gospel, in which King Herod orders the murder of all male children under two years old after hearing from the Magi of the birth of Christ on their way to Bethlehem (see Matthew 2:16–18). Accordingly, Ghirlandaio depicts the massacre of the innocents in the background, while in the foreground he shows two halo-wearing glorified children, dressed in white yet still bearing their wounds, representing the first martyrs of Christianity.

At first glance, it may seem that the principal scene is so crowded that it becomes difficult to find the three Magi at all. Not only does the upper left show the story of Herod's cruelty to the innocents, but the background right shows the angel announcing the birth of the Lord to the shepherds abiding in the field. St. John the Baptist is shown as a grown man in the lower left, while St. John the Evangelist appears in the lower right as an old man. Three richly dressed men appear, including one in a large blue hat, members of the silk guild who funded the hospital, alive at the time the painting was made.

In the equivalent place on the left, a man dressed in black has been identified as Francesco di Giorgio Tesori, the priest who commissioned the painting, while Ghirlandaio provides a self-portrait immediately to the right. This conflation of past, present, and future is typical for Ghirlandaio, whose work still has a foot in the late Middle Ages with its highly symbolic painting tradition. This also highlights one of the unique features of Florence during the early Renaissance: While the care of orphans may have once been funded and administered exclusively by the Church, it was now financed by wealthy Christian merchants, whose commitment was not any less real but operated in a different realm—the earthly city. This new attention to the civic realm that cooperated with the Church is symbolized by two small background figures dressed in black behind the Virgin: On the left, a cleric in a religious habit represents the Church, while on the right, a man in an open-necked shirt represents the laity.

Amidst the busy scenes of sacred and secular history, the Virgin sits in perfect serenity, her right hand raised in a gesture of amazement at the attention being given to her child, while St. Joseph is shown as an old man kneeling over her right shoulder. The three Magi appear in prominent places, the first as a golden-haired youth standing to the Virgin's right, offering the Christ child a crystal chalice, which foreshadows the Eucharist. Kneeling at the Virgin's feet, a bald Magus with long white hair and beard kisses Christ's foot, receiving a blessing in return. To his right, the third of the Magi, in the peak of middle age, kneels with a hand on his chest and a golden container to offer gifts. Together, they represent not only wise men from the East who recognize the Savior, but also the four symbolic "ages of man": youth, maturity, and old age, with Christ representing infancy. Though the idea of the four ages traces back to the ancient Roman poet Homer, Christians used this image as a way of contemplating the transience of life and the preparation for the eternal life that the birth of Jesus makes possible. Finally, the link between heaven and earth made possible by the birth of the God–Man is signified by singing angels holding a scroll of accurate Gregorian chant. Reading *gloria in excelsis Deo*, or "glory to God in the highest," it shows the celebratory song of the angels mentioned in the Gospel of Luke (2:14).

Ghirlandaio's *Adoration of the Magi* is not intended to portray a literal picture of this historical event. Christ's Incarnation occurred at a particular point in history, and the details are central to the Christian revelation. In great Christian art, though, the truth being conveyed is more important than the "facts"—meaning, the plan of God, presented sequentially or not, is meant to be known to the viewer in its fullness, rather than with historical accuracy. For an orphanage full of motherless children, the consoling image of a loving mother no doubt offered real consolation. But the conflating of past and present together with heaven and earth gives every Christian a reason to hope: God became man so that we might share in God's own divine life.

Celebrating the
Epiphany of the Lord

The Epiphany is the source of inspiration for many artistic contributions, notably Shakespeare's play *Twelfth Night*, which is centered on a party on the eve of Epiphany. A merry Roman celebration of the feast day is also the subject matter for the last movement (Epiphany) of Ottorino Respighi's orchestral work *Roman Festivals*. The celebration of the twelve days of Christmas that run from the Nativity of the Lord to the Epiphany is full of traditions for the home. While the secular world seems to believe that the Christmas season runs from November 1 to December 25, Catholics celebrate from the evening of December 24 until the feast of the Presentation of the Lord on February 2. Therefore, many families keep their Christmas tree up and decorations lit until this day.

The Journey of the Magi

In many cultures, there are special customs to celebrate this journey, such as the Spanish tradition of setting out baskets of hay to feed the camels of the wise men when they pass by the house.[17] Shoes are left out, hoping the Magi will return their thoughtfulness with a gift. An ancient Italian legend is often retold in the time leading up to Epiphany: the legend of Befana (or Bofana, from the word *Epiphania*). The story goes that Befana was too busy with her household duties to offer hospitality to the three wise men, insisting that she would not be so busy when they returned. The Magi left and never returned, but she continues to watch for them every Twelfth Night. Legend has it that she will fill the socks and shoes of the children with toys that night, as an encouragement for the children to be on their best behavior and hospitable to the three Magi.

Other cultures incorporate a gift exchange, saving one little treasured gift for this feast day. This is symbolic not only of the gifts of the Magi, but of the gift of the Christ-child to all of us (see Isaiah 7:14, 9:16; Matthew 1:23). Consider this simple custom, which Catholics of any age can appreciate: To commemorate the journey of the wise men from the East, position the Magi in your Nativity scene so that they journey from one end of the home to the other throughout the twelve days. Gradually move them closer to the crèche so that they arrive on the Epiphany, concluding with your family dinner prayer, sharing a gift or treat together.

One delicious custom is the baking of a special cake, which takes many different forms around the world. Whether it is the French tradition of baking a *galette des rois*, a puff-pastry tart made with almond paste or fruit, or the Spanish *rosca de reyes*, jam tarts and fruitcakes, most have one element in common: a small bean or almond is baked into the cake. Perhaps the most familiar is the King cake from New Orleans, an iced pastry or brioche ring decorated with bright colors of green, gold, and purple. There is one delightful surprise hidden inside: a tiny figure of the baby Jesus. Tradition holds that the person who discovers this figurine, or the bean, hidden in their slice becomes king or queen for the day. In some places, it also means you must host the celebrations the following year!

Epiphany House Blessing

Of all the traditions surrounding Epiphany, the blessing of homes is a treasured tradition among many Catholics. With the use of blessed chalk, the letters C+M+B are surrounded by the numbers of the current year on the doorframe or above the door, after the traditional names of the wise men: Caspar, Melchior, and Balthasar. There is also a popular interpretation of this inscription as an abbreviation of the Latin phrase *Christus mansionem benedicat* ("May Christ bless this house"). The *Directory on Popular Piety* indicates that the cross is the Cross of salvation, and that the blessing "expresses the blessing of Christ through the intercession of the three wise men."[18] This blessing is often accompanied by a family procession throughout the home, sprinkling each room with holy water. The complete order of blessing is often available from your parish along with blessed chalk, or can be found in *Catholic Household Blessings and Prayers*,[19] concluding with the following prayer:

> Lord God of heaven and earth,
> you revealed your only begotten Son
>   to every nation
> by the guidance of a star.
> Bless this house
> and all who inhabit it.
> Fill us with the light of Christ,
> that our concern for others may reflect your love.
> We ask this through Christ our Lord.
> Amen.

A Liturgical Calendar

During Mass on the Solemnity of the Epiphany, there is an unusual moment when, following the Gospel, the deacon proclaims an announcement of the date of Easter and the movable feasts of the year. The Epiphany proclamation dates prior to a time when we could easily look online for the date of Easter or purchase a printed calendar with the feast days laid out for us. Today, it is a much richer symbol than a simple calendar reminder. This proclamation brings the entire liturgical year into focus around its high point: the celebration of the Easter mysteries. To bring this ancient tradition home, consider planning your family calendar together during the weekend of Epiphany, making use of a liturgical calendar or ordo to help. In the United States, the USCCB publishes the "Announcement of Easter and the Movable Feasts" online each year. Is your family's year laid out on the central axis of Easter? Note the upcoming feast days, your family's name days, patron saints, and baptismal anniversaries. As a reminder of the gifts of the Magi, contemplate the gift of family prayer as you ask: *How can we devote more time to our domestic church in the new liturgical year?*

St. Joseph, Spouse of the Blessed Virgin Mary

March 19

Faith is the assurance of things hoped for, the conviction of things not seen.
For by it the men of old received divine approval.

–Hebrews 11:1–3

As the author of Hebrews tells us, faith is "the assurance of things hoped for, the conviction of things not seen" (11:1). Faith makes real—today—that which we have hoped for: God's loving plan for his people. In addition, faith gives us certainty about things we may otherwise be unsure of. "Assurance" and "conviction" are strong words that describe a firm faith in God.

The "men of old" mentioned in the letter to the Hebrews read on the Solemnity of St. Joseph exemplified such solid faith in the Lord. Abel, for example, offered to God the best of what he had. Who would do such a thing without faith? Noah built an enormous boat based on the word of God and a warning about what was not yet seen (see Hebrews 11:1). Similarly, Abraham had faith in God's promises, believing that God would give him a child. He also believed that, even if he offered up his son Isaac in sacrifice, "God was able to raise [Isaac] even from the dead" (Hebrews 11:19). Abraham also believed that God would make a great nation out of his descendants. In each case, these "men of old"—Abel, Noah, and Abraham—could see by the eyes of faith what to the human mind remained invisible, indeed, *un*-believable.

The first reading for the Mass doubles down on the strength of the ancients' faith in the person of David. The message from God's mouth to David's ear through Nathan's voice is that the all-powerful King David is, in fact, powerless to establish a dynasty or build any legacy to God. Rather, only when David is dead will God make manifest his promise by building a house and kingdom in David's name. "Trust me," God says; "I do," David responds. "Faith is the assurance of things hoped for, the conviction of things not seen."

Now enter St. Joseph, whom the Litany of St. Joseph calls "most faithful." Consider all the remarkable revelations in God's plan that Joseph was called to accept and follow on faith. His betrothed was pregnant—he knew not by him but was told by divine intervention. He is told to travel to Bethlehem during the final weeks of Mary's pregnancy, only to have her give birth to God in a stable. Wise men arrive to worship his newborn Son. At the Presentation in the Temple, Simeon predicts that this infant will be the downfall of many powerful men. Herod seeks to kill his child, so he is told to flee to Egypt. St. Joseph lives through each of these remarkable events with faith—he trusts that the unseen plan of God will play out in visible terms in real time. Who among us would accept with such assurance and conviction that all of these events were part of God's plan?

In the Office of Readings for this solemnity, St. Bernadine of Siena says that through St. Joseph's fidelity, "the Old Testament finds its fitting close. He brought the noble line of patriarchs and prophets to its promised fulfillment. What the divine goodness had offered as a promise to them, he held in his arms." Indeed, the nations foretold to Abraham, the protective ark delivered to Noah, and the royal house promised to David all come to fruition in this faithful descendant of David—a carpenter of Nazareth named Joseph.

Not only does today's Liturgy place St. Joseph squarely in the line of the faithful Old Testament figures—Abel, Noah, Abraham, David—but it also establishes Joseph as head of their long-awaited household. The entrance antiphon for his solemnity commands us to "Behold, a faithful and prudent steward, whom the Lord set over his household." The preface for the Mass recalls that St. Joseph "was given by you as spouse to the Virgin Mother of God and set as a wise and faithful servant in charge of your household to watch like a father over your Only Begotten Son." For those who find themselves dwelling in the household of the Church, St. Joseph remains a "paternal majordomo"—guiding, loving, and interceding for those who dwell under its roof.

A final consideration of the glories of St. Joseph is rooted in his marriage to Mary. The day's celebration is not simply called the "Solemnity of St. Joseph," but the "Solemnity of St. Joseph, *Spouse of the Blessed Virgin Mary*." We may have heard how today's families ought to model themselves on the Holy Family. But how does a family with God for a Son, a sinless virgin for a mother, and a saint as special as St. Joseph live? While we may not know the day-to-day lives of such a family, we do know that they were a family of faith. And if "faith is the assurance of things hoped for [and] the conviction of things not seen," then we do not need to know all the specifics of how the Holy Family lived more than two thousand years ago. Rather, under the care and guidance of St. Joseph, we can assent to live as God wishes today, following his will and his teachings, so that we can live with his holy family forever.

St. Joseph, pray for us!

Marriage of the Virgin by Pietro Perugino
(c. 1500–1515) Musée de Beaux-Arts, Caen

Though St. Joseph is graced with many honorific titles—from Patron of the Universal Church to Terror of Demons—he is remembered in the Church year as "Spouse of the Virgin Mary." Relatively little is said about Joseph in the Scriptures, which record none of his words. We are told that he was a descendant of David, forced by the circumstances over fifty generations to work as a carpenter. But the image of Joseph as earthly father of Jesus and spouse of the Blessed Virgin has fascinated Christians over the centuries, who have pondered the life of the Holy Family.

Pietro Perugino was hired to paint the *Marriage of the Virgin* for the cathedral in Perugia, the Italian city which gave the artist his name, because this great church held a very important relic—the wedding ring of the Virgin Mary. Though Scripture provided Perugino very little for inspiration, he found his narrative in a longstanding tradition of illustrating this event from a second-century text known as the *Protoevangelium of James*.

The *Protoevangelium* is non-canonical text, originally written in Greek around the year 150. Though it was considered unreliable by Origen in the third century and condemned by several popes in the fifth, the stories it told remained in the imaginations of the faithful. Copies of the original manuscripts eventually informed the thirteenth-century *Legenda sanctorum*, a collection of tales also known as the *Golden Legend*, which included the marriage of the Virgin. Details vary among different renditions of the story, but common to all is that Mary was considered a remarkably holy child, raised in the Temple of Jerusalem from the age of three, consecrated to God, and fed by angels. By the time she became a young woman, Temple authorities believed it best to find her a husband, but her purity and holiness made it a difficult task to find a worthy spouse. To solve the conundrum, the high priest Zechariah dressed himself in priestly vestments and went into the Holy of Holies—the most sacred room of the Temple—and an angel instructed him to call the widowers of Judea to the Temple, each with his walking stick, and wait for a sign. At the appropriate time, Joseph's rod burst into bloom and a dove from heaven landed upon it. Despite his protestations that he was too old and she too young, Joseph became the spouse of the Virgin Mary.

Though the scene had been illustrated many times in the Middle Ages, Perugino's painting shows the interest of Italian Renaissance artists in the depiction of accurate classical architecture and idealized space through use of the single-point perspective. In perspectival design, things in the distance appear smaller, rise toward the horizon, and converge toward a central vanishing point, giving a flat panel the appearance of depth. Based on the inherited narrative, Perugino makes the Temple building itself a major feature of the painting.

Though the Bible describes the Temple of Solomon as rectangular, an octagonal building was built over the temple's foundations after its destruction in the year 70, an Islamic shrine known today as the Dome of the Rock. However, when Jerusalem was taken by crusaders in 1099, they turned it into a church known as the *Templum Domini*, or Temple of the Lord. In an ironic twist of fate, the Jerusalem temple from then on was frequently portrayed in art as a domed octagonal building.

The staircase of the Temple marks the midpoint of the painting, with important action and figures arrayed below. Joseph is shown as an old man, and therefore chaste, holding the flowering rod in his left hand as he places a wedding ring on the Virgin's finger with his right. The high priest stands in the center, holding both of their wrists, his elaborate headdress a speculative take on the biblical description of the priestly *mitznefet*, or turban, worn in Temple worship. Surrounded by her fellow Temple virgins, Mary straightens her ring finger, and her left hand draws her attention to her obvious pregnancy. According to the *Golden Legend*, after their betrothal but before they were married, Mary returned to her father's house while Joseph traveled back to Bethlehem to inform his household and to retrieve anything he might need. Upon his return to Jerusalem, he found the Virgin with child, and he considered breaking their betrothal because of apparent infidelity, a violation of the Law, which he deeply respected. Nonetheless, the Lord appeared to him in a dream, telling him to become the spouse of the Virgin since the child was conceived by the Holy Spirit. So the Virgin's pregnant belly in the painting reveals more than a simple narrative. Not hidden in shame, it speaks of the miraculous conception of Christ, the exalted mission of the Virgin Mary, and the truth of Joseph as a just man who both follows the Law *and* obeys the Lord.

The Temple of Jerusalem was known for its extensive courtyards, with only the priests allowed to enter the temple building itself. Accordingly, Perugino places small groupings of people throughout the background, growing smaller to indicate distance, a masterful use of the newly codified theory of perspectival design heightened by the pavement's lines, which converge as they recede into the distance. Except for one sad man sitting alone on the temple's steps, most of the groupings show the various widowers carrying their walking sticks, in clear conversation about why they were not chosen and what this marriage could mean. One suitor in particular stands behind Joseph, breaking his rod across his knee in obvious frustration about missing the chance to marry such a blessed woman, and thereby subtly acknowledging Joseph's special status as God's choice of spouse for the Virgin Mary and all that it would eventually involve: protector of the Holy Family, foster father of Christ, and paternal intercessor for Christians through all time.

Celebrating the Solemnity of St. Joseph

For many centuries, St. Joseph's life of virtue has been a model for Christians. This is reflected in the Church's official prayer and in the devotional life of the faithful. His virtues are numerous: "Faith, with which he fully accepted God's salvific plan; prompt and silent obedience to the will of God; love for and fulfillment of the law, true piety, fortitude in time of trial; chaste love for the Blessed Virgin Mary, a dutiful exercise of his paternal authority, and fruitful reticence."[20] Due to his importance in the life of Jesus, he is the patron of the universal Church, as well as numerous countries such as Canada, Mexico, and Poland. He is often depicted holding the carpenter's square, signifying both his craft and commitment to truth, and the lily, which symbolizes his purity.

Litany of St. Joseph

A common devotional practice on this solemnity is to pray the Litany of St. Joseph, which invokes the various titles of Joseph as the earthly father of Jesus and husband of Mary. In 2021, during the Year of St. Joseph, Pope Francis added an additional seven invocations to the Litany: guardian of the Redeemer, servant of Christ, minister of salvation, support in difficulties, patron of exiles, patron of the afflicted, and patron of the poor. In his apostolic letter *Patris Corde*, Pope Francis aimed to draw attention to the life of St. Joseph, in order "to increase our love for this great saint, to encourage us to implore his intercession and to imitate his virtues and his zeal."[21]

Fatherhood and Consecration

One of the aspects that Pope Francis emphasizes in his letter is the fatherhood of St. Joseph, describing him as a "beloved father," loving, accepting, obedient, and working. St. Joseph, as the earthly father of Jesus, is a model for all Christian fathers. One spiritual practice that many Catholic husbands and fathers undertake between March 19 and May 1 (the feast of St. Joseph the Worker) is to make a consecration to St. Joseph. This thirty-three-day journey is similar to the consecration to the Blessed Virgin Mary. It follows the various invocations in the Litany of St. Joseph. In this way, we recognize Joseph as our spiritual father and make a commitment to imitate him, asking him to help us along the path to holiness.

St. Joseph's Altar

La tavala di San Giuseppe ("the table of St. Joseph") is a popular annual custom that originates in Sicily. According to tradition, St. Joseph interceded to spare the people from famine following a terrible drought. The Sicilian people promised to honor St. Joseph with a feast if he would intercede on their behalf to God for the rain to come to end the famine. It is said that the fava bean is the crop that spared them from the famine following the rain. The St. Joseph altar is customarily elaborate: a large table of multiple tiers, full of foods, candles, medals, and figures. One prominent feature is the shaped bread in honor of this patron saint. The various shapes of bread include crosses, crowns of thorns, sheaves of wheat, symbols of St. Joseph himself, his staff, or even his beard! The spread is traditionally meatless, as this solemnity falls during Lent, but it does include sweets, such as *zeppole*. These little confections of fried choux pastry are filled with a custard-like pastry cream and topped with a cherry, specially made for this feast day. The tradition of the St. Joseph's Table is more than a work of art, as it truly becomes a community celebration —food is shared with all and no one turned away, as those who have more share with the less fortunate.

Prayer to St. Joseph

In 1885, Pope Leo XIII approved the prayer *A te, Beate Joseph* as a daily recitation for the faithful in popular devotion. It carries with it a partial indulgence.[22] On this solemnity, let us pray for the intercession of St. Joseph as we imitate his life of virtue:

> To you, O Blessed Joseph, do we come in our tribulation, and having implored the help of your most holy Spouse, we confidently invoke your patronage also. Through that charity which bound you to the Immaculate Virgin, Mother of God and through the paternal love with which you embraced the Child Jesus, we humbly beg you graciously to regard the inheritance which Jesus Christ has purchased by His Blood, and with your power and strength to aid us in our necessities. O most watchful Guardian of the Holy Family, defend the chosen children of Jesus Christ. O most loving father, ward off from us every contagion of error and corrupting influence; O our most mighty protector, be kind to us and from heaven assist us in our struggle with the power of darkness. As once you rescued the Child Jesus from deadly peril, so now protect God's Holy Church from the snares of the enemy and from all adversity; shield, too, each one of us by your constant protection, so that, supported by your example and your aid, we may be able to live piously, to die in holiness, and to obtain eternal happiness in heaven. Amen.

The Annunciation of the Lord

March 25

God, the author of all, knows how to write a good story. The Bible communicates a single message of redemption, what some have called an enormous love letter from God to his beloved people. Yet throughout the rich variety of poems, prayers, narrative, and song, there is a unifying theme. Each word, each verse, and each book of the Bible hangs together to execute this theme—as we might expect from God, whose identity is, after all, the "Word." Today's solemnity, the Annunciation of the Lord, celebrates one of the most profound moments in Scripture's rich tapestry and illustrates the integrity of the revealed Word in remarkable ways.

Today's celebration of Gabriel's message to Mary and her affirmative reply recalls the events from the very first verses of the Bible. In the book of Genesis, Eve is tempted by the devil, the Father of Lies, to close her ears to God's life-giving Word. Despite God's command that our first parents were not to eat from the tree of the knowledge of good and evil, "the woman saw that the tree was good for food, and that it was a delight to the eyes, and that the tree was to be desired to make one wise, [so] she took of its fruit and ate; and she also gave some to her husband, and he ate" (Genesis 3:6). We know the rest of the story—and we know it is true because we have lived with the consequences of the Fall in our lives.

With this initial chapter of the "greatest story ever told" in mind, consider now the approaching apex of God's letter, the appearance of the angel Gabriel to Mary. The ancient hymn *Ave, Maris Stella* gives us an interpretive key to the scene. It sings of how the first word of Gabriel to Mary, *Ave*, transforms the damage, confusion, detours, and dead ends along the road to heaven wrought by Eve, in Latin, *Eva*. St. Irenaeus (c. 130–202) sees the same reversal at this turning point of salvation history: "As Eve was seduced by the word of an angel and so fled from God after disobeying his word, Mary in her turn was given the good news by the word of an angel, and bore God in obedience to his word. As Eve was seduced into disobedience to God, so Mary was persuaded into obedience to God; thus the Virgin Mary became the advocate of the virgin Eve."[23] Thus, the celebration of the Annunciation of the Lord first recalls with gratitude that *fiat*, "let it be done," from Mary that brought God to man, heaven to earth, at Christmas.

The Annunciation and the Nativity are the two great celebrations of the coming of God to earth. Together, they serve as essential chapters in God's narrative of salvation. Mary, after conceiving Christ "through her ear," that is, by listening to and receiving God's message, gives birth to this same Savior nine months later.

Naturally, the Church marks the celebration of these two days nine months apart—the March 25 incarnation of the Word comes to fruition with the Savior's birth on December 25. These two dates also find a ritual association unique to themselves: during the recitation of the Creed, at the words "and became man," all present genuflect or kneel rather than merely bowing, as on other occasions. Since eternity "grounds itself" in our time, since divinity unites itself to our humanity ("human," from *humus*, or "earth," "dirt"), we humans likewise bend our knees and, literally, ground our own selves.

The Church's liturgy, though, does not simply recall the historical annunciation and birth of Jesus nine months later, but it also directs our attention to his death and resurrection. Before March 25 celebrated Jesus' conception, it was on this day that the Church recalled his death. In the early centuries of the Church, March 25 corresponded roughly to 14 Nisan on the Jewish calendar, the day of Passover, which is when Christ the Paschal Lamb was slain. The God–Man would suffer death for our salvation as a result of Eve's disobedient "no" and Mary's obedient "yes."

In some ways, the Annunciation celebrates the Paschal Mystery as much as it does the Incarnation. As St. Leo's text from the day's Office of Readings puts it, "Incapable of suffering as God, he did not refuse to be a man, capable of suffering. Immortal, he chose to be subject to the laws of death." But the Paschal Mystery is not only about Christ's suffering and death but also his resurrection. The liturgy of the Church ties the Annunciation to the Resurrection in the Prayer after Communion at Mass, asking that by "confessing that he who was conceived of the Virgin Mary is true God and true man, we may, through the saving power of his Resurrection, merit to attain eternal joy."

The Annunciation of the Lord, then, serves as a pivotal event in this largest of love letters. Just days before Christmas, St. Bernard of Clairvaux (1090–1153) paints a vivid picture of our emotions as we overhear Gabriel's announcement and await Mary's reply. It is an image that expresses beautifully the significance of Mary's choice on this day. He writes: "Answer quickly, O Virgin. Reply in haste to the angel, or rather through the angel to the Lord. Answer with a word, receive the Word of God. Speak your own word, conceive the divine Word. Breathe a passing word, embrace the eternal Word … Let humility be bold, let modesty be confident. This is no time for virginal simplicity to forget prudence. In this matter alone, O prudent Virgin, do not fear to be presumptuous … *Behold the handmaid of the Lord*, she says, *be it done to me according to your word*."[24]

Murate Annunciation by Fra Filippo Lippi
(c. 1440–1445) Alte Pinakothek, Munich

Jesus does not appear in an obvious way in Fra Filippo Lippi's *Murate Annunciation* or in any of the other seven versions of the same event he painted in his lifetime. But the central mystery of Christianity—that the Word of God became flesh—underpins every one of them. Each reveals how God planned from the beginning of time for the Virgin's womb to be a spotless home for Christ. So while the scene speaks profoundly of Mary as the privileged recipient of God's grace, it expresses even more profoundly that every glory given to the Virgin is a share in the glory of Christ and God's plan for salvation. She is immaculate because Christ made her so, and her womb is special because he prepared it as his chosen dwelling place in the world.

Rightly, then, biblical "types" abound and find completion in the Virgin. As mentioned previously, a "type" is a prophetic figure or symbol, often an idea in the Old Testament that points to its fulfillment in the New. The story of Jonah and the great fish, for instance, prefigures Jesus' time in the tomb and subsequent resurrection. Similarly, the high priest in the Temple foreshadowed Christ the true High Priest, as the letter to the Hebrews makes clear. A figure as central as the Virgin is also foreshadowed typologically. She is called the *porta clausa*, the "closed gate" through which only the Lord could pass since she remained forever a virgin (see Ezekiel 44:2). For similar reasons, she is the *hortus conclusus*, or "enclosed garden," a place of delight unsullied by corruption where Christ could dwell (see Song of Songs, 4:12). Additionally, she is the *templum Domini*, or "temple of the Lord," since her body is the place where God chose to dwell with his people. And lastly, she is the palace of God since she provides a home for Christ, the king, to dwell in her womb. Though Lippi's *Annunciation* may first appear as a simple telling of a biblical event, he layers the painting with visual images of these rich Scriptural ideas, giving it a theological depth in addition to visual beauty.[25]

Filippo Lippi's personal life is frequently described as "colorful," a fitting artistic pun for both his life and his work. Orphaned at age two, he grew up in a monastery of Carmelite friars, received a classical education, and was eventually ordained a priest. He left religious life without permission, eventually fathering two children. Some claimed he had once been abducted by pirates, others that he was locked up by his powerful patrons and forced to paint, only to escape by a rope made of bed sheets. He was frequently impoverished, involved in lawsuits and even forgery, but his artistic talent appeared to overwhelm his questionable morals. As the 1903 *Catholic Encyclopedia* entry on Lippi scathingly puts it, "Talent placed its possessor beyond and above the moral law." Nonetheless, the Church put his artistic talents to work to reveal the Blessed Virgin as purest of the pure.

The Annunciation marks the moment when the archangel Gabriel announces that the Holy Spirit will conceive the Savior in the Virgin's womb. The angel greets her with the phrase "full of grace," which theologians have pondered ever since as a sign of her Immaculate Conception and unique preparation to give flesh to Christ. In a telling move, Lippi makes Gabriel, whose name in Hebrew can translate as "strong man of God," kneel before Mary. Her "yes" indicates her own strength as Mother of God, even as her pose indicates that she has just stood in surprise, with her modesty evident in her downward glance. Gabriel offers her an extraordinarily large stem of lilies, while a second angel in the doorway appears with another. Though the lily is long known as a sign of Mary's purity, a stem this size harkens back to Isaiah 11 and its prediction of the savior as the flower of a great rod from the tree of Jesse, and also Aaron's rod, which blossomed without water or soil just as the Virgin conceived without a natural husband. God the Father appears surrounded by angels in the upper left, sending the dove of the Holy Spirit toward Mary on golden diagonal rays.

An elaborate background contrasts with the simplicity of the figures, the setting an erudite palace with architectural details only recently re-learned in the Italian Renaissance's quest to recover the standards of ancient Rome. The Virgin's womb will soon become the home of Christ the King, and so the "palace" which is the Virgin's womb is expressed in her exterior surroundings. Large Corinthian columns, distinguished by their capitals rich with acanthus leaves, which have signified unmarried women since antiquity, mark arches supported by scrolled Ionic columns, which in turn signify maternity. So the place is more than a marker of status. It also speaks of the nature of Mary, who is soon to be both virgin and mother. Through the colonnade appears a walled garden with no gate, combining two allusions to the Virgin's womb. In the prophet Ezekiel's great vision (see Ezekiel 40–43), he sees a temple built without human hands into which God's glory rushes through the east gate.

So God's Presence has returned to his Temple, an apt allusion for Christ, who returns to the temple of Mary. The angel told Ezekiel that this gate must remain shut, since the Lord God had entered through it, echoing Isaiah 7:14: "The Virgin will conceive and bear a son." The enclosed garden, an image expressed by King Solomon to his bride in the Song of Songs, now becomes fulfilled as a song of Christ, the new Solomon, to his bride the Church, all typified by the Virgin Mary. So enclosed garden and palace come together in the Virgin Mary, a typological fulfillment only heightened by the pillar which appears in the center of the garden, which has traditionally been associated with Mary since columns marked places of importance, and therefore her singular role in salvation history.

Celebrating the Annunciation of the Lord

The Angelus by Jean-François Millet

Examining the history of this solemnity reveals that the date of the Annunciation was first mentioned in the sixth century. It was fixed to March 25 to correspond both with Our Lord's Nativity as well as the date of his passion. According to a certain tradition, it is also the day on which the great Flood is said to have begun, though its specific date is not recorded in the Bible. It was at the Council of Ephesus in the year 431 that the teaching authority of the Church decreed Mary to be *Theotokos* ("God-bearer")—that is, the Mother of God.

Marian Overtones

This solemnity, while celebrating the Incarnation of the Lord, is rich in Marian overtones due to her vital importance in this moment of salvation history. It is because of her "yes" at the Annunciation that "the Word was made flesh and dwelt among us." This feast day is rich in an abundance of devotional prayers for the home with a particular Marian emphasis. One of the simplest acts on this day is to pray the Joyful Mysteries of the Rosary, as the first joyful mystery is the Annunciation. The Rosary is called "one of the most excellent prayers to the Mother of God,"[26] as a contemplative journey through the saving events of Christ accompanied by his blessed Mother. Pius XII even described the Rosary as the "compendium of the entire Gospel."[27] The Joyful Mysteries follow the journey through the Annunciation, birth of our Lord, and his young life. It is fitting that this day's Rosary intentions are offered for expectant mothers, those who struggle with infertility, and those facing crisis pregnancies.

Praying the Angelus

In the tradition of the Church, the faithful would pray this pious exercise recalling the announcement from the angel Gabriel to Mary at three times of the day—dawn, midday, and dusk. Often, church bells were rung in an extended pattern, known as "ringing the Angelus," at 6:00 a.m., noon, and 6:00 p.m. The pattern comprises nine strokes in total, consisting of three triple strokes and pausing between each group. It is usually followed by a peal or nine additional bell tolls. While this specific pattern does not appear to be decreed at any point in time, this usage is a widely followed tradition. Many Catholic schools retain this practice at the lunch hour, pausing for a few moments of the day to remember the Incarnation as a pivotal moment in salvation history. In this technological age, it is not unheard of for people to set their phone alarms to mark out these moments of the day—with the sound of church bells, of course. During his pontificate, St. John XXIII began the practice of the Sunday Angelus address, when the pope speaks to the faithful in St. Peter's Square from the window of the apostolic palace. This short exhortation is followed by the *Angelus* (or *Regina Caeli* during the Easter season) and concludes with a papal blessing. In his apostolic exhortation *Marialis Cultus*, St. Paul VI writes that the Angelus remains ever popular in the piety of the faithful due to "its simple structure, its biblical character, its historical origin which links it to the prayer for peace and safety, and its quasi-liturgical rhythm which sanctifies different moments during the day, and because it reminds us of the Paschal Mystery."[28] In the midst of all of the activities of the daily life of work, school, and family obligations, the *Angelus* provides a moment's rest to stop and nourish our lives with prayer, contemplating the mystery of the Incarnation, in any day and age.

Praying the Magnificat

Every evening at evening prayer, the Church bursts forth into the song of Mary, taken from Luke's Gospel (see Luke 1:46–55). The three great canticles of the liturgical day—the Canticle of Zechariah in the morning, the Canticle of Mary in the evening, and the Canticle of Simeon at night—all flow from the mystery of the Incarnation. Mary's song, the Magnificat, is her song of joy to the Lord following the events of the Annunciation and her subsequent visit with Elizabeth. "My soul magnifies the Lord, and my spirit rejoices in God my Savior" (Luke 1:46–47). Praying the Magnificat on this day, we recall her *fiat* as the Holy Spirit plants Our Lord into her heart.

In *The Admirable Heart of Mary*, St. John Eudes describes Mary's heart as a "garden of delights," the paradise of the new Adam, and a new Garden of Eden. This image of paradise is one that we can imitate in a small yet significant way. Depending on the gardening zone in which you live, March 25 is an ideal time to start seeds or to plant spring flowers for your Mary garden, which can be a place of prayer on Marian feast days throughout the year, such as the month of May, August 15 (the Assumption), or September 8 (the birth of Mary). There are many botanical associations for Our Lady which can be adapted to the home garden or table. St. Bernard of Clairvaux highlights the virtues of Mary in floral imagery: "the violet of humility, the lily of purity, and the rose of charity. She is the rose that flowers bearing the Christ-child: 'O Mystic Rose of fragrance sweet, thy beauty brings us Christ to meet.'"[29]

Waffle Day

To honor that sweetness of Mary, there are some fun ways to incorporate liturgical living to celebrate the Annunciation. One perhaps surprising gastronomic custom on this feast day comes from Sweden, where waffles are eaten. Apparently, this delightful tradition comes from a play on words, arising in the seventeenth century, due to the similarity in Swedish between *Vårfrudagen* ("Our Lady's Day") and *Våffeldagen* ("Waffle Day").[30] On this solemnity, then, it is customary to feast on a sweet treat in honor of Mary as we celebrate Our Lady's day.

Easter

First Sunday following the first full moon of the vernal equinox

Exult, let them exult, the hosts of heaven, exult, let Angel ministers of God exult, let the trumpet of salvation sound aloud our mighty King's triumph!

–Opening verses of the Easter Proclamation, the *Exsultet*

Easter is the "solemnity of solemnities"; it is the supreme celebration of our Catholic Faith. This solemnity of the Resurrection of the Lord is so fundamental to our faith that it is not limited to a single day, but lasts eight days (an octave), from Easter Sunday to Divine Mercy Sunday. The Easter season extends over an octave of Sundays, a period of fifty days, ending on Pentecost. Truly, there is much to discuss about this great solemnity, from fires and fonts to candles and chrism. But underlying each liturgical and devotional prayer is the Paschal Mystery of Jesus.

The Paschal Mystery is Jesus' suffering, death, resurrection, and ascension, by which he *passed* (the meaning of the Hebrew word *pascha*) from the fallen world of sin back to the eternal world of the Father. By these saving, priestly actions, Jesus bridges heaven and earth so that those who follow him can access divine life. This Paschal Mystery is the content of all things Easter.

If we limit our focus to that high point of Easter, the Easter Vigil, we can see how Christ's saving work is revealed in the Vigil's four principal movements: the Service of Light (or *Lucernarium*); the Liturgy of the Word; the initiation of new Christians in the sacraments of Baptism and Confirmation; and the celebration of the Eucharist.

The Service of Light includes the blessing of the Easter fire, procession into the church, and the singing of the *Exsultet*, or Easter Proclamation—which together express the Paschal Mystery in signs, symbols, and poetry. Much of the entrance rite's meaning comes from the first Passover out of Egypt more than three thousand years ago, when Moses led God's enslaved people out of a land of darkness and death into the promised land of freedom. Through his saving Passion, Jesus Christ fulfills what Moses anticipated and what we today recall: He battled the devil, passed through death, and rose victorious to the Father's right hand. The Service of Light makes Christ's Paschal work, prefigured by Moses, present in sacramental signs: the thurible creates a pillar of smoke; the paschal candle leads as the true pillar of fire; the priest guides us like Moses; we, as God's people, pass from the cold and dark and ignorance of night into warmth, light, and knowledge of eternal light in the body of the church. Then, much as Moses and the Israelites "sing to the Lord, for he has triumphed gloriously; the horse and his rider he has thrown into the sea" (Exodus 15:1), the new Moses and the new People of God sing God's praise in the *Exsultet*: "O truly blessed night, worthy alone to know the time and hour when Christ rose from the underworld!"

The Liturgy of the Word proclaims the Paschal Mystery in inspired language. During this "mother of all holy Vigils," as St. Augustine calls it, nine Scripture readings are prescribed: seven from the Old Testament, one from the letter of Paul to the Romans, and a Gospel passage that announces Christ's resurrection. "Thus," say the liturgical directives concerning this part of the Vigil Mass, "the Church, 'beginning with Moses and all the prophets,' explains Christ's paschal mystery."[31] It is noteworthy that, even though some of the seven Old Testament readings can be omitted "where more serious pastoral circumstances demand it,"[32] the Church requires that the story of the Exodus out of Egypt be proclaimed since it is the solemnity's fundamental theme—the passing over from death to life.

The initiation sacraments of Baptism and Confirmation communicate the Paschal Mystery of Christ with water and oil. Much like the entrance rites and the Liturgy of the Word before it, there are numerous details that each play their part in presenting Christ and his Paschal Mystery to the Church in our time. At the heart of Baptism and Confirmation, though, we see men, women, and children adopted into and strengthened in their life of faith by joining themselves to Christ's own suffering, death, resurrection, and ascension. Like him, they prepare for battle with temptation and evil. With Jesus, they die to themselves and rise to new life.

If Baptism and Confirmation provide the entrée, however, the celebration of the sacrament of the Eucharist offers the main course by presenting the Paschal Mystery in a truly substantial way. In the Upper Room on Holy Thursday, when Jesus celebrated the Last Supper with his apostles, the body and blood of the sacrificial meal *reached ahead* to his Good Friday sacrifice upon the Cross, making that sacrifice present in their midst. Upon the altar at the Easter Vigil (and at every Mass), the Church, through the power of the Holy Spirit, *reaches back* to that same saving sacrifice upon Golgotha. Therefore, Christ's sacrifice is present at every Mass so we can join our own individual sacrifices—prayers, works, joys, and sufferings—to his ultimate sacrifice. With Christ, we offer ourselves, mind and heart, body and soul, to the Father in the Holy Spirit. Those who give themselves most fully in the Eucharist are then able most completely to pass over.

This great solemnity of Easter is not only the supreme celebration of our faith but also the fulcrum for all other celebrations. This day stands at the center of the Church year. All other celebrations prepare for it, and all observances extend it. It is a bridge connecting all the truths of the Faith and our present life to the one to come.

The Resurrection of Christ by Raphael
(c. 1499–1502) São Paulo Museum of Art, São Paulo, Brazil

In his first letter to the Corinthians, St. Paul makes an extraordinary claim: "If Christ has not been raised, then our preaching is in vain and your faith is in vain" (1 Corinthians 15:14). Christ's resurrection means that his humanity—and therefore all of humanity—is no longer subject to death as the result of the sin of Adam and Eve. Christ took on humanity to join it to divinity, and he entered death to destroy it forever. So Paul's claim is not exaggerated. Without the resurrection of Jesus, every other promise of Christianity is for nothing. Raphael's *Resurrection of Christ*, painted when he was only sixteen, captures both the magnificence of the event and its larger meaning in salvation history, all the while demonstrating his prodigious talent and his signature artistic serenity.

Unlike some later representations of the Resurrection that show explosive power and dynamic energy, Raphael gives the event a kind of tranquil stillness, even as guards fall to the ground and angels announce this cosmic event. Jesus hovers peacefully above his own tomb, no longer limited by earthly gravity, dressed in a royal garment trimmed in gold to mark his divinity. Yet his earthy fleshliness, including the wounds on his hands, feet, and side, remains on display as his bare chest and exposed abdomen proclaim his glorified humanity. He holds a flowing white flag with a red cross, traditionally understood to signify his victory over death. Some scholars have noted that this flag is a battle standard known as an *oriflamme*, used in the Middle Ages when a king led an army against the enemies of Christianity. This small flag, then, marks not only the victory of the Resurrection itself but also the battle that Christ will wage in the Church through history to defeat Satan and his armies.

Raphael represents Christ's tomb not as a rustic cave but as a *sarcophagus*, a large stone coffin common in the ancient world whose name literally means "flesh eater." Though the tomb's lid has been lifted and its interior is clearly empty, its front reads like an altar, and the curved central feature on the lid presents itself as a pedestal. Art historian Charles Stewart has proposed a connection between the resurrection of Christ and the Holy Eucharist, where the sacred host is elevated above the altar to receive the gaze of the faithful and be beheld as the first fruits of humanity's glorious restoration. In Raphael's painting, Christ is similarly suspended, showing his glorified Body and offering its resurrected glory for the life of the world. Fittingly, this image once appeared immediately behind an altar, so the liturgical action of the Mass and the biblical reality of Christ formed one theological whole.

Though Raphael gives the work a certain composed stillness, scholars frequently note the choreographic quality of his figures and the strict geometry which guides their placement. Christ fills the central vertical axis, his body contrasted with the light sky behind, and his feet mark the horizontal midpoint of the painting, organizing the image into four quadrants by the shape of a cross. Though clearly in awe of the event, the four guards around the tomb form four corners of a rectangle, thought by some to signify the four corners of the earth, as foretold by Isaiah, who prophesied that Christ would "gather the dispersed of Judah from the four corners of the earth" (Isaiah 11:12).[33] Their poses read like a frozen ballet as their arms and gazes lead the viewer's eye to Christ with an effortless gracefulness that typified Raphael's work in the High Renaissance. The feet of the angels clearly defy gravity, and they simultaneously look down to the guards and point to heaven, forming two diagonals that lead directly to Christ's face. A group of three women holding jars appears in the middle ground, a reference to Mark 16, which notes that Mary Magdalene, Mary the mother of James, and Salome came to the tomb to anoint Christ's body, only to be shocked to find the tomb empty. Tucked closely together, they form a small square according to a proportional module one quarter of the height of Christ's body and one third the width of the tomb. By composing the painting upon a reasoned geometric framework, Raphael gave the image a perfection based on the order of numbers and mathematics, the antidote to the chaos of the fallen world.

An artist such as Raphael, even while still a teenager, paints with numerous levels of meaning, making a painting worthy of close inspection. The altar is made of white, green, and red marble, signifying the virtues of faith, hope, and charity infused into Christians and made possible by the Passion of Christ. A red-crested crane appears on the right, a bird mentioned in Scripture (see, for example, Isaiah 38:14, Jeremiah 8:7). Known for its piercing voice and long life, it became a symbol of loyalty and resurrection because of its lengthy migrations and sure return each spring. Cranes are also adept at eating snakes, one of which Raphael placed prominently at the lower left corner. The crane, then, invites the viewer to ponder Christ as the new Adam who defeats Satan, undoing the serpent's apparent victory over the first Adam. And in one easily missed tableau, a spring appears to the left of the altar, watering a white Easter lily. The water, necessary for both ordinary life and the new life of Baptism, nourishes the hidden lily bulb, which, in the fullness of time, rises up from the ground in shining glory, just as Christ rose from the tomb. Raphael's *Resurrection*, then, shows how God's plan of salvation runs through all of creation, from the glory of Christ's body to birds of the air and plants of the earth. Together, all of creation sings God's praise and heralds his offer of grace to all who desire it.

Celebrating Easter

As the crowning point of the liturgical year, it should be no surprise that the Easter celebration has inspired countless devotions around the world. Both traditional customs and new practices highlight the glory of the Resurrection and Christ's triumph over sin and death. The customary Easter greeting: "Christ is risen, alleluia!" and its reply: "He is truly risen, alleluia!" (or "He is risen indeed, alleluia!") appears in myriad languages and cultures. The other traditional Easter greeting comes from Psalm 118: "This is the day which the LORD has made!" with its reply, "Let us rejoice and be glad in it, alleluia!"

Fount of Life

At the Easter Vigil, the water for Baptism is blessed with a beautiful prayer that retells the story of water in salvation history. Many families bring specially decorated containers or even simple jars to the church to take holy water to their home from the Easter font. Some parishes even provide small containers to collect the blessed Easter water or have a holy water font from which parishioners can obtain holy water at any time during the year. Holy water in the home can be kept in a font near the door for making the Sign of the Cross upon entering and leaving the house. As St. Teresa of Avila writes, "There is nothing like holy water to put devils to flight and prevent them from coming back again. They also flee from the Cross, but return; so holy water must have great virtue. For my own part, whenever I take it, my soul feels a particular and most notable consolation. In fact, it is quite usual for me to be conscious of a refreshment which I cannot possibly describe, resembling an inward joy which comforts my whole soul."[34]

Blessing of Foods

On Holy Saturday morning, or early on Easter morning, there is a special custom of blessing the first foods which will be eaten, "the first meal of Easter, when fasting is ended and the Church is filled with joy."[35] This special blessing is celebrated in many parishes, where families bring highly decorated baskets full of Easter eggs, bread, chocolates, and other delights. In some cultures, it is the custom to bless wine, whereas in others, bread takes the central place.

Bread of Life

In Ukrainian tradition, several foods are prepared ahead of Holy Saturday for the blessing of Easter baskets. These include eggs, ham and sausage, butter, cheese, horseradish root, salt, special breads called Paska and Babka, and Pysanky (Easter eggs). *Paska* is a braided bread that is prepared especially for this feast day, described as a work of art. Easter breads are an important reminder of the gift of Christ in the Eucharist, as found in this beautiful theological insertion in one recipe: "The Paska in the Easter basket reminds us that Christ is the Living Bread."[36] Mothers and daughters pass on the tradition of braiding these breads with twists, crosses, roses, and doves. Many Eastern European cultures celebrate with sweet Easter breads that are rich in symbolism, often exquisitely decorated, and full of rich ingredients like butter, milk, and of course, sugar.

Easter Eggs

Another food included in the Easter baskets of many cultures is the Easter egg, often intricately decorated and dyed. According to some accounts, this tradition dates to the thirteenth century. The egg, a symbol of new life, also represents the end of the Lenten fast. In a letter from St. Gregory the Great to Augustine of Canterbury, he writes that Christians of that time abstain not only from meat but from anything that comes from "the flesh" including eggs, cheese, and butter. The eggs for Easter were decorated and then eaten during the feast following the fast.[37] There are many unique egg traditions around the world: egg tapping in Greece, an egg dance in Germany, eggs filled with confetti (*cascarones*) in Latin America, or the elaborate waxing and dying of Ukrainian *pysanky*.

The Light of Christ

A completely darkened church is a striking symbol at the beginning of the Easter Vigil. When the deacon carries the paschal candle in procession and its single flame spreads to illuminate the entire building, "bringing light, warmth, and hope," this candle is "a symbol for the Christian of the rising Christ, who is the true Light of the world."[38] A new custom that is catching on is the practice of a "Holy Week of Darkness," where a family avoids the use of artificial light in their home during Holy Week, using only the light of candles. It certainly is a unique sacrifice to do this for an entire week! Then, after the Easter vigil, the "truly blessed night," the children run around the house turning on every light to symbolize and celebrate the glory of the Resurrection.

Divine Mercy

During the octave of Easter, the faithful are invited to contemplate more deeply the mercy of God, remembering the mercy that poured forth from the wounded side of Jesus on the Cross. The Divine Mercy devotion was given to St. Faustina in an apparition by our Lord, and the novena is prayed for the nine days preceding the Second Sunday of Easter (Divine Mercy Sunday), beginning on Good Friday. The Chaplet of Divine Mercy can be prayed using rosary beads. Many families have the traditional image of the Divine Mercy in their home, the red and white rays emanating from the side of Christ representing the blood and water that poured forth from his side. As Our Lord told Faustina, "The pale ray stands for the Water which makes souls righteous; the red ray stands for the Blood which is the life of souls." The message of Divine Mercy is spread to the whole world on this day. Celebrating this devotion during Easter week reminds us of Psalm 89 with joy, "I will sing of your mercies, O Lord, for ever."

The Ascension of the Lord

Traditionally celebrated on a Thursday, the fortieth day of Easter

Moved to Sunday in some regions

The solemnity of the Ascension comes forty days after the "main event" of Easter. This might be why it has the sense of being somewhat of an afterthought to the Paschal Mystery. In addition, in the Church's post-Vatican II liturgical calendar, the Ascension has been reduced from its status of an octave to a single day, which might also have caused the faithful's appreciation of it to wane a bit. Then there is the fact that it has been transferred in many places from being celebrated on the fortieth day of Easter, Ascension Thursday, to the Seventh Sunday of Easter, reducing its status to "just another Sunday" to many. Nonetheless, the Ascension remains one of the four constitutive parts of the Paschal Mystery, along with Jesus' suffering, death, and resurrection.

The letter of the Hebrews (an excerpt of which may be used as the second reading for the Mass on the Ascension) explains how Jesus' return to his heavenly Father is an integral part of the Paschal Mystery. In the Old Testament, the Chosen People's high priest had to offer bulls and goats each year on the altar of the Temple. But each of these—the high priest, the animals, the altar, and the Temple—were mere shadows and anticipations of Christ, the true High Priest, his Body and Blood the true offering, the true altar which is the Cross, and heaven the true sanctuary. As the reading explains, "Christ has entered, not into a sanctuary made with hands, a copy of the true one, but into heaven itself, now to appear in the presence of God on our behalf" (Hebrews 9:24). His offering is "once for all" (Hebrews 9:12). For this reason, he is called the "great priest over the house of God" (Hebrews 10:21). The ascension of Jesus "above the highest heavens" (Entrance antiphon) concludes his sacrifice, represents its acceptance by the Father, and completes the construction of the paschal bridge from earth to heaven.

The Ascension opens the way for us to follow Jesus. As the same passage from the letter to the Hebrews explains, "we have confidence to enter the sanctuary by the blood of Jesus, by *the new and living way* which he opened for us through the curtain, that is, through his flesh" (10:19–20; emphasis added). The liturgy for this solemnity tells us that if we are members of his body, the Church, then we can—indeed, must—follow where the head leads us, just as our own head and body travel and arrive together. The preface for the Mass during the Eucharistic prayer recalls that Christ "ascended, not to distance himself from our lowly state but that we, his members, might be confident of following where he, our Head and Founder, has gone before." The patristic text from the Office of Readings of the day comes from a St. Augustine homily for the same feast. Its main point is an ecclesial one: "the body as a unity cannot be separated from the head." Indeed, as we hear in the Eucharistic prayer, we even hear how we share a place at the Father's right hand: "your Only Begotten Son, our Lord, placed at the right hand of your glory our weak human nature, which he had united to himself."

The Ascension of Our Lord, then, celebrates not only the completion of Christ's Paschal Mystery, but also the opening of heaven's gates to those joined to him in Baptism. As the third-century theologian Origen put it, "The divine Word promises much greater and more lofty things to you who have passed through Jordan's stream by the sacrament of baptism: he promises you a passage even through the sky."[39] Likewise, St. Leo the Great, writing in the fifth century, imagines what the apostles themselves thought as they witnessed Christ's ascension: "[T]hat blessed company had a great and inexpressible cause for joy when it saw man's nature rising above the dignity of the whole heavenly creation, above the ranks of angels, above the exalted status of archangels. Nor would there be any limit to its upward course until humanity was admitted to a seat at the right hand of the eternal Father, to be enthroned at last in the glory of him to whose nature it was wedded in the person of the Son."[40]

The Solemnity of the Ascension celebrates the great possibilities that lie ahead of us. But we know, too, that this same gift of godliness described by St. Leo—what the Church calls "divinization"—is not one we must wait to open but are to live today. As Pope Benedict describes it, living the divine life is not only "life after death, in contrast to this present life, which is transient and not eternal. 'Eternal life' is life itself, real life, which can also be lived in the present age and is no longer challenged by physical death."[41] As Christ arises, then, riding that highway in the clouds (see Psalm 68), we should strive to ride along with him, for the Solemnity of the Ascension is another marker on our road to eternity.

The Ascension of Christ by Benjamin West
(1801) Denver Art Museum

In one sense, Benjamin West's *Ascension of Christ* is a straightforward depiction of the sacred event when Jesus enters the true sanctuary of heaven. But creating the painting involved an unlikely set of circumstances. Though painted for King George III's royal chapel at Windsor Castle, it was nonetheless rendered by Benjamin West, a Pennsylvania-born American Quaker with no formal training in art. West is known in art history as one of the first Americans to leave the New World and study art in Europe, making an in-depth study of Greek and Roman antiquities. A prodigious talent, he settled in England, entering the circles of British clerics, artists, and intellectuals. He even became acquainted with the king, with whom he had discussions on the state of art in England and the formation of a Royal Academy of Art. West would go on to become the academy's president and historical painter to the king, while Buckingham Palace eventually featured many large canvases painted by West's hand.

Largely known as a history painter, West excelled at depicting ancient Greece, scenes from Shakespeare, Native Americans, modern war heroes, and even leaders of the American Revolution. But his body of work also includes significant religious paintings, largely scenes from Scripture. But rather than make paintings layered with sacramental symbolism as Raphael might have done three centuries earlier, the "American Raphael," as West was called, was clearly under the sway of *historicism*, a post-Enlightenment understanding of the authoritative value of history. Accordingly, his figures drew heavily and often literally from the precedent of Greek statuary. West wrote to a fellow painter that "the form of man has been fixed by eternal laws" but that the ancient Greek art produced figures that "leave no room for improvement."[42]

The Ascension of Christ is more than four feet tall, a highly finished study for a final painting intended for King George III's Chapel of Revealed Religion, an unbuilt project planned in the late eighteenth century. A subtle but important feature of this sacred image is its *historical* character. While a painter in the Italian Renaissance would happily paint a scene of Christ's ascension, he would have depicted it as outside of time, emphasizing the sacramental meaning of the event over its details. The political and religious situation in England meant that anything which smacked of "popery" was decidedly unwelcome, so much so that the bishop of London refused to allow paintings to be added to St. Paul's Cathedral. King George, however, could make decisions about his own personal chapel, and he approved West's deeply biblical and historical vision proposing dozens of paintings portraying the history of Christianity as God's revelation. Nonetheless, the king had the proposed list of subjects approved by various Church leaders so that Christians of all Protestant denominations could ponder the paintings without violating their beliefs.

An early drawing shows the *Ascension* as the central and largest painting in a group of five Old and New Testament scenes, showing the historical event as a marker of Christ's divinity and fulfillment of scriptural revelation. In some ways, it can prove difficult to provide symbolic interpretation for works that had to be "safe" enough to avoid offense. In addition to the Protestant unease about figural images, the eighteenth century was a time of historic*ism*, a philosophical system seeking to understand and explain social and cultural belief systems by studying the process of their historical progression. While a fifteenth-century Catholic painter might present a scriptural scene as a jewel-like artwork rendering present the glories of heaven, a historicist painter saw authority as coming primarily from the evidence of history. One art historian has rightly noted that the paintings for West's proposed chapel are a "prime example" of this historicist approach, desiring to reveal the historical progression of Christianity and its origins, therefore providing for the moral and religious edification of the people.[43]

West's painting aptly captures the dramatic moment in the first chapter of the Acts of the Apostles, showing Christ bathed in light and surrounded by small baby-like angels known as *putti*. He organizes the painting along a strong diagonal that runs from bottom right to top left, with a powerful contrast between the light of heavenly glory and the relative darkness of earth below. Acts mentions that Christ was lifted up "and a cloud took him out of their sight" (Acts 1:9). Clouds appear throughout Scripture as a sign of God's presence and power, and so West indicated Christ's divinity by showing him raised by a cloud like an elevator. The onlookers appear suitably astonished, with their aquiline noses and ballet-like poses decidedly recalling the ancient Greek statues that West admired. Two winged angels dressed in white—one apparently male and the other female—appear on the right, simultaneously pointing to Christ and addressing the people below. Here, West accurately follows the scriptural narrative in which angels said to the crowd: "Men of Galilee, why do you stand looking into heaven? This Jesus, who was taken up from you into heaven, will come in the same way as you saw him go into heaven" (Acts 1:11).

West's *Ascension* aptly reveals how sacred art remains deeply intertwined with the complexities of human history in addition to theology. While traditional in representation and deeply biblical, it becomes a foil to the Catholic imagination, which presents sacred historical events as active realities in our own time rather than merely edifying events worthy of memory. Rather than depict the transfigured saints of the future—and therefore its current relevance as a living liturgical reality—West merely painted sacred history, satisfying the theological and philosophical restrictions placed upon him.

Celebrating the Ascension of the Lord

During the first three centuries, the Ascension of the Lord was commemorated with the coming of the Holy Spirit on Pentecost. In the mid-fourth century, it arises as a separate feast day and achieves nearly universal spread by the fifth century. This solemnity is mentioned among the important feasts and mysteries of the Lord by the Church Fathers, especially St. Augustine and St. John Chrysostom. In Chrysostom's homily on the Ascension, he brings it into eschatological focus for mankind: "Through the mystery of the Ascension we, who seemed unworthy of God's earth, are taken up into Heaven."[44]

Climbing the Mountain

At Byzantine Vespers on Ascension Thursday, we hear this excerpt: "Come you, O faithful, and let us climb the Mount of Olives and with the Apostles let us lift up our minds and our hearts on high. Let us behold our Lord as He is taken up to heaven and let us cry out with joy and gratitude: Glory to Your ascension, O most merciful One."[45] If you are blessed to live in a geographic region where climbing a mountain or hillside is possible, take part in this common central European tradition for this feast day. As sacramental beings, we turn to natural symbols like mountains, water, and fire, as signs of spiritual events. These signs point us toward the sacred mysteries. A hilltop hike or journey to a mountain for a picnic is a reminder of the scriptures of the day, commemorating Christ's ascent at the Mount of Olives.

For the Birds

For a festive dinner on this feast day, it is customary to eat some type of bird, such as a pheasant, quail, or goose. German tradition serves pastries in the form of various birds. This calls to mind various images of Jesus "flying" up to heaven. Some churches used an oculus in the ceiling (see Pentecost for more on that tradition) to draw up a statue of the risen Lord through the opening, leaving worshippers staring up at the heavens as in the Bible: "Men of Galilee, why are you standing there looking at the sky? This Jesus who has been taken up from you into heaven will return in the same way as you have seen him going into heaven" (Acts 1:11).

Rogation Days

One ancient English custom for this feast day was called "Beating the Bounds." This tradition marked out the parish boundaries by making a formal procession around them while carrying boughs or branches, hitting various signposts along the way (trees, stones, other markers).[46] There is a relationship between this tradition and the procession for the blessing of crops which customarily occurs during the Ascension rogation days, which were marked with fasting and prayer. (The word *rogation* is from the Latin "to ask.") The three days before Ascension are called "minor rogation days." On these days, Christians would fast, pray litanies, and process through the fields to bless crops, avoid damaging pests, and pray for good weather. Today, there are special votive Masses that can be prayed for these agricultural intentions.

The Via Lucis

While most Catholics are familiar with the Stations of the Cross, or *Via Crucis*, many are surprised to learn about its lesser-known relative, the *Via Lucis*, or Way of Light. This is a stational prayer that resembles the Stations of the Cross, but instead of following the steps of Christ on the way to Calvary, it centers on the Gospel appearances of Christ following his resurrection to his ascension (see Matthew 28, Mark 16, Luke 24, John 20). The origins of this practice come from ancient Christian devotion which has been revitalized and formalized in recent years. It is inspired by an ancient inscription at the catacombs of St. Callistus. The Holy See promotes this devotion in the *Directory on Popular Piety and the Liturgy*, praising it as "an excellent pedagogy of the faith, since '*per crucem ad lucem* ["through the cross to the light"].' Using the metaphor of a journey, the *Via Lucis* moves from the experience of suffering, which in God's plan is part of life, to the hope of arriving at man's true end: liberation, joy and peace which are essentially paschal values."[47] This perfectly summarizes the two facets of the Paschal mystery, which the *Catechism* recalls, that "by his death, Christ liberates us from sin; by his resurrection, he opens for us the way to a new life" (CCC 654). Each station of light follows a familiar pattern from the stations of the cross, with an Easter twist emphasizing the Resurrection:

> We adore you, O Christ, and we praise you!
> Because by the Wood of the Cross and the
> Light of the Resurrection:
> You have redeemed the world!

Pentecost Novena

The Novena to the Holy Spirit begins today. Between the Lord's ascension and the coming of the Holy Spirit, the disciples "joined in continuous prayer, together with several women, including Mary the mother of Jesus, and with his brothers" (Acts 1:14). Similarly, the Church spends the nine days preceding Pentecost praying for the coming of the Spirit. This is the true origin of this novena as a practice in Christian piety, one of the earliest forms of intercessory prayer. In the family, one way to simply incorporate a novena is to pray it after dinner. To extend the liturgical life to the family, it is especially appropriate to celebrate Evening Prayer from the Liturgy of the Hours during these nine days. As we await the promised comforter, the Paraclete, let us pray for the Holy Spirit to renew our hearts and help us to be open to God's will.

Pentecost Sunday

The fiftieth day after Easter

The solemnity of Pentecost brings the Easter season to a close. Jesus, after suffering, dying, rising, and ascending to the Father's right hand, sends the gift of the Holy Spirit to seal and confirm his work. In history, the sending of the Spirit at Pentecost ushered in a new age. At this moment, the apostles, cowering in fear, were given new life—and new gifts—to carry out the great commission that Christ had given them at his ascension. In the liturgy, too, Jesus gives to us a special outpouring of the Spirit so that we, like so many before us, can carry out our baptismal mission to proclaim the good news.

There are many dimensions to the singular gift of the Holy Spirit at Pentecost. In fact, the Solemnity of Pentecost requires numerous liturgies for its celebration. Most solemnities use a single set of readings and prayers for the celebration of their vigil and daytime Masses. Others, like the Ascension, have one set of prayers for the vigil and a different set for Mass during the day. Pentecost, though, not only has Mass prayers and readings for the vigil and Sunday Masses, but also has special readings, texts, and rituals for an *extended* Vigil, one not unlike the Easter Vigil celebrated fifty days earlier. This extended vigil for Pentecost—which contains four readings, as well as the option to incorporate Evening Prayer—imitates the urgent prayer of Mary and the apostles as they awaited the Advocate. And when the Spirit comes, he inspires those with hearts and souls receptive to him in five ways: through breath, fire, intoxication, water, and rejuvenation of soul.

The Gospel reading for the day's Mass recounts Jesus' appearance to the apostles in the locked room following his resurrection. Standing in their midst, "he breathed on them, and said to them, 'Receive the Holy Spirit'" (John 20:22). The Spirit is the "breath" of God. Fifty days after his resurrection, a second breath of Spirit will come upon the apostles as a "rush of a mighty wind" (Acts 2:2). For this reason, at the Chrism Mass, the bishop, who stands in Christ's place as high priest, consecrates the sacred chrism used in Confirmation by breathing into the vessel, so that its oil becomes a sacramental means of bestowing the "sacred Breath." Similarly, Pentecost breathes new life into souls wearied from sin.

This new life, though, is not simply a restoration to life in the Garden before the Fall. On the contrary, the Spirit ignites those who receive it and inflames them to a higher state of sanctity than even our first parents possessed. One line of thought found in the tradition sees the Holy Spirit flowing from Christ's open side upon the Cross as a "river of fire." Later, as the Acts of the Apostles recounts, the Holy Spirit comes upon the apostles in "tongues as of fire" (Acts 2:3).

To this day, Catholics pray, "Come, Holy Spirit, fill the hearts of your faithful and kindle in them the fire of your love."[48]

The account of the Holy Spirit descending at Pentecost describes how each apostle, now on fire with the Spirit, begins speaking in tongues. Before it became a Christian feast, Pentecost was a pilgrimage feast for the Jews, which is why there were in Jerusalem Chosen People from different lands. But when the apostles speak, the pilgrims are amazed, for they hear them speaking in their own languages (see Acts 2:11). Note that a skeptic in the crowd, upon hearing this strange talk, scoffs, "They are filled with new wine" (Acts 2:13)—and he may have been correct. As a sixth-century author explains, "Some people were not far wrong in saying: *They have been drinking too much new wine.* The truth is that the disciples had now become fresh wineskins, renewed and made holy by grace. The new wine of the Holy Spirit filled them, so that their fervor brimmed over and they spoke in manifold tongues."[49] Christian language is characterized by both sobriety (of Jesus) and inebriation (of the Spirit).

"Sober inebriation" is not the only paradox on this day, for the fire of the Spirit is accompanied by the Spirit as moisture. In the Office of Readings for this solemnity, St. Irenaeus (130–202) explains how the devil, burned by being thrown down like lightning, seeks to incinerate us: "If we are not to be scorched and made unfruitful, we need the dew of God. Since we have our accuser, we need an Advocate as well." Similarly, Irenaeus likens us to dry flour waiting to be baked and fired into a loaf. But flour needs water to become bread. "Like dry flour, which cannot become one lump of dough, one loaf of bread, without moisture, we who are many could not become one in Christ Jesus without the water that comes down from heaven."[50]

Finally, and as consequence of receiving the Holy Spirit as breath, fire, wine, and water, the Holy Spirit also gives us a "new" soul, *anima*, making us divine sons and daughters of the heavenly Father. St. Paul tells us in a reading for the Mass that those "who are led by the Spirit of God are sons of God" (Romans 8:14) and, consequently, "we may also be glorified with him" (Romans 8:17). Possessing the Spirit of God—or, rather, *being possessed by* his Spirit—makes us divine. Our first parents sinned by wanting to be like God, but according to their own plan. Now, we are made like God according to his plan and his power.

Pentecost bestows many blessings on the Church and her members. For those who receive the Spirit as breath, fire, inebriation, water, and soul, divine life becomes a reality on earth.

Pentecost, folio 79 from the *Très Riches Heures du Duc de Berry*, by Jean Colombe
(c. 1485–1490) Musée Condé, Chantilly, France

Jean Colombe's representation of Pentecost enriched one of the most famous manuscripts of all time, a book of hours known as the *Très Riches Heures of Duc de Berry*. A book of hours holds a collection of psalms, prayers, and readings to be prayed at different times of the day. Building on the Jewish tradition of praying at the Temple at regular intervals, the early Church brought this pattern into her official liturgy, today known as the Liturgy of the Hours. Meant to allow the faithful to ponder the riches of the Mass across morning, afternoon, and night, the prayers paralleled the liturgical seasons and saints' days. By the late Middle Ages, the art of making these prayer books rose to remarkable standards of beauty in calligraphy and painted illustration, but the *Très Riches Heures*, as the name reveals, was perhaps the most elaborate of all, commissioned by the Duc de Berry, son of French King John II. Painted over the span of more than one hundred years, the result was 416 handmade pages and 131 painted images amidst illuminated letters and rich borders, now considered one of the finest artistic achievements in western history.

Many of the book's illuminations were painted between 1412 and 1416 by the Limbourg brothers, three famous miniaturists from Holland who worked in France, and who died—together with the duke—in 1416. In the 1480s, the Duke of Savoy acquired the unfinished work and asked Jean Colombe, an experienced miniaturist, to continue the project. At first glance, Colombe's rendition of the moment when the Holy Spirit descends upon the Virgin and the apostles to give birth to the Church is almost secondary to a dizzying complexity of architectural richness. The elements of the biblical narrative are there, with the disciples arranged in a circle below the dove of the Holy Spirit, whose golden light illuminates their faces and clothing. The Virgin Mary appears at the center, slightly larger than the others, the only one shown with a halo. But Colombe makes the room, which Scripture simply describes as a "place," into a richly decorated hall filled with multi-colored columns and an array of statues. While he most likely did not have accurate archaeological knowledge of the architecture of ancient Jerusalem and so resorted to a kind of imaginative reconstruction, he was likely embodying the theology of the Church as "God's building" (1 Corinthians 3:9) composed of "living stones" built into a spiritual house (1 Peter 2:5). So rather than try for archaeological accuracy, the image reveals theological truth about the Church, made of many members who now act in one accord as the Church, thanks to the Holy Spirit.

Columns and stones are extremely common themes in Scripture, though they are frequently overlooked. Christ's body is explicitly compared to the Temple in Jerusalem (see John 2:21), and the Temple was famous for its array of perfectly cut stones. The Temple was the place of God's dwelling with his creation, and therefore Christ is the new and perfect Temple who seamlessly joins both human and divine natures. Later Paul would write of the Church as Christ's body, made of many members with different functions assembled under his headship (see Romans 12:4–8). Moreover, the Bible speaks frequently of columns as the architectural rendition of people, notably in Exodus where they represent the twelve tribes (24:4) and in Galatians 2:9 where Peter, James, and John are called "pillars." This description of the Church as both Christ's body and God's building came over time to be blended into artistic renderings where they appear as one.

Colombe's room features six colored columns which seem to hollow out as they move to the top, giving the impression that the figures they support are not so much hanging *on* the columns as inhabiting them. This visual duality might easily be interpreted as a kind of architectural naiveté, but it reveals Scripture's poetic interpretation of "pillars" as saints, as people who are as integral to the Church as structural columns are to a building. Moreover, their varying colors—red, gray, and blue—speak not only of the colored marbles of ancient Jerusalem but also of the different functions of the many members of the body. The walls behind exhibit similar properties. A close look reveals a church interior perforated by windows, but the center section shows them crowded almost to invisibility, as if the walls are really statues of saints, prophets, and angels, and the need for natural light is a secondary concern. Here the symbolic value of the living stones trumps the need for a literal representation of actual stones.

Colombe's paintings are recognizable by their golden *trompe l'oeil* frames, and *Pentecost* has the same theological pattern, appearing, like the painting, to be formed of living stones. Produced with light brown paint and gold highlights to imitate the appearance of gilded wood, the frame is edged with clustered columns composed of small, winged angels and various saints. Across the bottom of the frame, five unidentified figures appear, many wearing exotic headdresses, suggesting that they may be images of Old Testament forerunners of Christ. Beneath them is written the beginning of the line from Psalm 51 with which the Liturgy of the Hours opens: "Lord, open my lips, and my mouth will proclaim your praise." The line takes on a second meaning for Pentecost, since one of the gifts of the Holy Spirit given was the ability to tell the mighty works of God in many languages, with the lips of Galileans now opened to bring the message of Christ to the world.

The Duc de Berry's book of hours aptly "sacramentalizes" this same voice of Christ in the world. More than simply a collection of words, its decorated letters and magnificent illustrations add a fascinating glory to the text, much as the Transfiguration added radiant glory to the Incarnation. Through the hand of the artist, the spoken word becomes more and more like the Word spoken by the Father, drawing Christians to the work of prayer, and allowing prayer to raise them up to God.

Celebrating Pentecost

Pentecost, in the early church, was a term that often referred to the whole fifty-day season following Easter. It is also known in some places as Whitsunday, because of the white garments worn by the newly baptized, who continue their sacramental mystagogy throughout these weeks. This period is influenced by the Jewish festival known as the Feast of Weeks, seven weeks after Passover. It originally celebrated the harvest and later was a reminder of Moses receiving the Law at Sinai. In Christian liturgical time, this number of fifty days is significant—it is a week of weeks, plus one day. It is a surplus of time, in the same way an octave (eight days) indicates super-abundance. The joy of the Resurrection spills over not just one week into a surplus but overflows a week of weeks.

Fire and the Holy Spirit

On this day, we recall the descent of the Holy Spirit upon the apostles in the form of tongues of fire. Romano Guardini describes this fire as "the aptest symbol we have for the soul within that makes us live."[51] We pray for the Church in a particular way on this day, which is often referred to as the birthday of the Church. The apostles received the seven gifts of the Holy Spirit, which we also receive in the sacrament of Confirmation—wisdom, understanding, counsel, fortitude, knowledge, piety, and fear of the Lord. These gifts enabled the apostles to preach the Gospel to great effect, and on that first Pentecost, they converted more than three thousand to Christ. Some families celebrate the birthday of the Church with a cake, especially one featuring fruits like strawberries to represent the fruits of the Holy Spirit.

Roses Are Red

Red has long been associated with the descent of the Holy Spirit, reminiscent of tongues of fire, as well as the burning fire of the love of God. Traditionally, churches are adorned with red roses on this solemnity, which led to nicknames such as *Pascha Rossatum* (Pasch or Feast of Roses). In some places, Catholics have traditionally worn (at least some) red on this feast day and decorate their homes with red as well.

In the Church of St. Mary and the Martyrs in Rome, red rose petals are dropped from the oculus in its dome. This is a powerful image reminiscent of tongues of fire descending upon the apostles. Many medieval European churches had a round hole in the ceiling which was known as a "Holy Ghost hole." During the celebration, a carved figure in the form of a dove would be lowered through the hole to symbolize the descent of the Holy Spirit. The feast became famous for more dramatic symbolism in some parts of the world, as choristers would imitate the sound of rushing wind with hissing and blowing noises as the dove was lowered, or live doves were even released in the church. In other places, short pieces of straw lit on fire were dropped through this hole. Today, while the custom of the rose petals continues in Rome, you may notice a more subdued reference in many domed churches: at the height of the dome on the interior, the central circle features the figure of a dove.

Sing Alleluia

The evening of Pentecost Sunday marks the last day for singing the *Regina Caeli* (Queen of Heaven), which is the Marian antiphon for the Easter season. This chant is a great starting point for families wishing to learn to sing together from the great treasury of the Church's tradition and would usually be sung before going to sleep after praying Night Prayer. Young children especially love singing the alleluias at the end of each phrase. You can easily find a recording of this chant or the sheet music for it to learn it together, finishing your family evening prayer with the *Regina Caeli* to mark the end of the Easter season. There are four short sung phrases that are traditionally followed by a short verse and response, and a concluding prayer:

V. *Regina caeli, laetare, alleluia.*
R. *Quia quem meruisti portare, alleluia.*
V. *Resurrexit, sicut dixit, alleluia.*
R. *Ora pro nobis Deum, alleluia.*

V. Queen of heaven, rejoice, alleluia.
R. For he whom you did merit to bear, alleluia.
V. He has risen, as he said, alleluia.
R. Pray for us to God, alleluia.

V. Rejoice and be glad, O Virgin Mary, alleluia.
R. For the Lord has truly risen, alleluia.

Let us pray. O God, who gave joy to the world through the resurrection of Thy Son, our Lord Jesus Christ, grant we beseech Thee, that through the intercession of the Virgin Mary, His Mother, we may obtain the joys of everlasting life. Through the same Christ our Lord. Amen.

Come, Holy Spirit

One of the prayers most associated with this day, Come, Holy Spirit can be used at any time. This prayer is a wonderful way to begin a school day, a meeting, or any group activity. Ask the Holy Spirit to fill your life with new spiritual gifts in this coming year:

Come, Holy Spirit, fill the hearts of your faithful and kindle in them the fire of your love. Send forth your Spirit, and they shall be created. And you shall renew the face of the earth. O, God, who by the light of the Holy Spirit, did instruct the hearts of the faithful, grant that by the same Holy Spirit we may be truly wise and ever enjoy his consolations, through Christ Our Lord. Amen.

The Most Holy Trinity

The first Sunday after Pentecost

Blest be God the Father, and the Only Begotten Son of God, and also the Holy Spirit, for he has shown us his merciful love.

–Entrance antiphon, Solemnity of the Most Holy Trinity

When you pray, to whom do you address your prayers? To God the Father? To God the Son? To God the Holy Spirit? Or to God in general? There is no wrong answer to this multiple-choice question. However we might answer, it should get us thinking about the mystery of the Most Holy Trinity: what it is and why it matters to our life in the Faith.

The truth of the Trinity is expressed in Scripture. Hints of this three-part mystery open up the story of salvation in the Bible's first verses: "In the beginning God created the heavens and the earth. The earth was without form and void, and darkness was upon the face of the deep; and the Spirit of God was moving over the face of the waters. And God said, 'Let there be light'; and there was light" (Genesis 1:1–3). In this passage, God the Father creates by speaking his Word, God the Son, and by the breath of God the Holy Spirit.

At the high point of salvation history, from the Cross on Calvary, God again reveals himself as Trinity: "Jesus, crying with a loud voice, said, 'Father, into your hands I commit my spirit!' And having said this he breathed his last" (Luke 23:46). God the Son announces his self-offering to God the Father by the breath of God the Holy Spirit (see CCC 730).

The Trinity also closes the Scriptures and completes all things: "The book of *Revelation* … first reveals to us, 'A throne stood in heaven, with one seated on the throne': 'the Lord God.' It then shows the Lamb, 'standing, as though it had been slain': Christ crucified and risen … Finally it presents 'the river of the water of life … flowing from the throne of God and of the Lamb,' one of the most beautiful symbols of the Holy Spirit" (CCC 1137). As Father, Son, and Spirit create all things in the beginning and redeem all things in the middle, so the Trinity concludes all things at history's end.

Based on the Scriptures, Christians have sought to understand this greatest mystery of our Faith. Consider, for example, how each of us has a thought, image, or idea of who we are as individuals. This image may be an accurate representation of the original, or it may be significantly distorted. But however true to form the thought that we human thinkers have of ourselves may be, it always falls short. God the Father, though, does not have this problem! When he considers himself, this thought, idea, and image is the same as he, the thinker—they are "consubstantial," as the Council of Nicaea articulated in 325. The only difference between Thinker and Thought is one of origins: the Father begets the Son. And as Father and Son relate to one another, the bond of love between them is similarly substantial. The Father pours himself out to and for the Son, and the Son pours himself out to and for the Father—and that outpouring between them is the Holy Spirit. For the Holy Trinity, the lovers and the love they express for one another are substantially the same. Each—Father, Son, and Spirit—is God, and all are one God.

Our finite human minds cannot truly understand the nature of the infinite God. That said, various theologians have offered analogies that can help us grasp certain aspects of the Trinity. Pope Benedict XVI likens the Trinity to a conversation where the "Father eternally utters his Word in the Holy Spirit … God himself [is] the dialogue of love between the divine persons."[52]

Another tradition is expressed, "In the secret of his life, God chants unto himself an eternal hymn which is nothing else than the expression of his perfections in his Word and in the Breath of his Love."[53] The first reading for Mass on this solemnity from Proverbs speaks of the "Wisdom of God," which the Church Fathers see as the Son, delighting the Father and "rejoicing before him always, rejoicing in his inhabited world" (Proverbs 8:30).

Given our limited ability to understand the nature of the Trinity, what should this foundational belief of our Faith mean for us in our spiritual journey? The solemnity of the Most Holy Trinity teaches us that all three divine Persons—Father, Son, and Holy Spirit—are at work in everything and at all times (see CCC 258). It is the Father, Son, and Spirit who create us; it is the Father, Son, and Spirit who save us; it is the Father, Son, and Spirit who sanctify and divinize us—each according to his own Person, but each in unity with the others. Consequently, we are in contact with each divine Person, and each loves us, communes with us, and fills us with the divine life. As the *Catechism* puts it, "The whole Christian life is a communion with each of the divine persons, without in any way separating them" (CCC 259).

Our prayer and life as Christians, then, is essentially Trinitarian. We are made in the image and likeness of the three Persons of God (see Genesis 1:26); we love and adore them as one God. As the text of the Preface of the Mass for this solemnity says, "In the confessing of the true and eternal Godhead, you [are] adored in what is proper to each Person, their unity in substance, and their equality in majesty." Even our lives should resemble the Trinitarian communion. Like each of the divine Persons, we are blessedly unique; and like each Person, we live in love and communion with others.

At the first moments of the world's creation, the Trinity was present. At our baptism, the Trinity was there, as we were baptized in the name of the Father, and of the Son, and of the Holy Spirit. In heaven, the Trinity is present for all eternity. The Solemnity of the Most Holy Trinity recalls the life-giving moments of our past and gives a glimpse of eternal life to come. In so doing, it also reminds us that all of creation, all of existence—every moment of salvation history—is characterized by the Trinity's expressive, inexpressible love.

Christ died for all 2 Cor. 5:15

Central Panel, Mural at the Cathedral of the Madeleine, by Felix Lieftuchter
(c. 1918) Salt Lake City

In a 1918 renovation of Salt Lake City's Cathedral of the Madeleine, the bishop and his architect decided to do something that would be unthinkable today—they removed, and possibly destroyed, five Bavarian stained-glass windows depicting the Sorrowful Mysteries of the Rosary. They then filled in the window openings and unified the church's interior with a mural depicting a vision of heaven and its celestial inhabitants. While it may seem a small distinction, they transformed the primary art of the cathedral's interior from *devotional* art of the Rosary to *liturgical* art based on the nature of Catholic worship, which was then being rediscovered by theologians in the liturgical revival of the early twentieth century. They hired a talented young Cincinnati painter, Felix Lieftuchter, to fill the church with an uncommon—and Trinitarian—ensemble of glorified figures and gem-like color based on the biblical vision of St. John the Apostle.

The theological foundation for Lieftuchter's mural comes from the nature of Catholic worship and its foundations in Scripture, particularly the book of Revelation, in which St. John describes a vision of the worship of heaven. In Revelation 4, John sees the glorified Jesus in gem-like radiance surrounded by four winged creatures representing the four evangelists singing "holy, holy, holy is the Lord God almighty" and white-robed elders in similar adoration. Later, he sees a myriad of angels, as well as "every creature in heaven and on earth and under the earth and in the sea" (Revelation 5:13). In his final vision, John sees the new heaven and the new earth as a great garden surrounded by gem-covered walls where the servants of God see his face and delight in him forever (Revelation 20:10–21; 21:4). So heavenly worship is glorified, centered on God, and involves all of creation: not only the angels and saints, but the stars, plants, fish, and animals. This vision provides the theological foundation for the Mass, which is the earthly sacramental participation in the true worship of heaven.

In this context, the cathedral's murals prove more than mere pious ornaments, but the terrestrial vision of the invisible realities of heaven. Lieftuchter's crucifixion is therefore neither primarily a rendition of the historical event in Jerusalem nor a devotional image to help contemplate Christ's suffering. In the liturgical setting of the cathedral, it shows a glorified image of the eternal act of Christ offering himself with all of creation to the Father through the power of the Holy Spirit. Here, then, is a *liturgical* image, one which shows the reality of the liturgy itself and encourages worshippers to participate in Christ's priestly action. The mural proved prophetic; fifty years later, the documents of Vatican II would encourage the laity to participate in the liturgy "by offering the Immaculate Victim, not only through the hands of the priest, but also with him, they should learn also to offer themselves" (*Sacrosanctum Concilium*, 48).

Though little known today, Felix Lieftuchter left a legacy of great cathedral mural programs, including those in Toledo, Ohio, and Wheeling, West Virginia. In each case, he gave different versions of the heavenly city, but at the Cathedral of the Madeleine, Christ's cross is presented as the throne of his sacrifice for others. Though in some ways it resembles the historical crucifixion on Golgotha, Christ's offering is now heavenly and eternal. The cross is supported by the hands and the lap of the Father and, together with the Holy Spirit, forms a representation known as the "Throne of Mercy." This rendition of the Trinity was developed in the Middle Ages and shows the Father presenting Christ's sacrifice to the faithful to support the claim found in John 3:16 that God so loved the world that he gave his only begotten Son. Wearing a three-tiered Trinitarian crown, God the Father is surrounded by radiant glory and sorrowing angels who recognize the suffering of Christ. Two other angels in colorful heavenly dress catch the blood flowing from Christ's wounds, their feet in a vertical pose to show their weightlessness.

The golden walls of the heavenly Jerusalem appear in the background, confirming that Christ's self-offering occurs within heaven itself, unlike the historical crucifixion, which occurred outside the city's walls. The cloud-filled skies of earth appear behind the cross, while above the ceiling is decorated with cosmic stars of the glorified cosmos, marking the eternal radiance of the heavens. These two skies signify John's description of a new heaven and a new earth, each brought to glory. The stars above are now the stars of eternity, no longer the pinholes of light seen from earth, but exalted and restored, having flowered even beyond the glory God gave them before the Fall.

At the base of the cross appears a pelican feeding her young, a long-established analogy for Christ based on the belief that the mother pelican would pluck her feathers and feed her young with her own blood, just as Christ feeds the world with his Blood in the Eucharist. Here, too, the cross springs to life as a great vine, reiterating its reality as the new Tree of Life and swirling vine, a great image of the Church: Christ as the vine and its members as the branches. The visual cues reinforce the chosen Scripture quote from 2 Corinthians 5:15, reading not only "Christ died for all" as the mural displays, but which continues, "that those who live might live no longer for themselves but for him who for their sake died and was raised." Here the visual gospel matches the written gospel; each invites the worshippers to join their lives to the eternal sacrifice of Christ and share in his eternal glory.

The cathedral's mural, like all Christian art, remains deeply rooted in the revelation of Scripture, particularly the Incarnation, where Christ's material body showed that matter can reveal God to the world. Moreover, at the Transfiguration on Mt. Tabor, that same body became radiant with God's glory. A great liturgical mural grows from and displays the deep sacramental economy of Catholic worship, where God continues to make himself known to us through his own creation, which he contemplated and saw was good.

Celebrating the Solemnity of the Most Holy Trinity

The solemnity of the Most Holy Trinity is a prime example of a liturgical celebration that grew out of the devotional life of the Christian people. Popular piety of the Middle Ages featured many practices devoted to the Trinity, which is "the central mystery of the faith and of the Christian life" (CCC 234). Devotions and liturgical prayers were composed to reaffirm this mystery. In 1334, this liturgical feast was added to the general calendar in the Latin Church by Pope John XXII.

The Sign of the Cross

First among the symbols of the Trinity is that prayer which begins so many of our devotional and liturgical prayers—the Sign of the Cross. This prayer is extremely powerful, which is why it frames every prayerful act in our day. Great saints knew the power of this prayer. Legend is that St. Tibertius, who was condemned to death during the persecution of the Roman emperor Diocletian, made the Sign of the Cross over a blazing fire before walking through it unscathed.

The Sign of the Cross is the first action of the sacrament of Baptism, and it is the first sign given to catechumens in the liturgy. The Church claims the one to be baptized for Christ with this powerful sign on his or her forehead, which is the "imprint of Christ" (CCC 1235). Each time we make the Sign of the Cross, we are reminded of our baptism and declare we belong to Christ.

Many Catholic families have a holy water font by the door of their house and bless themselves as they pass by it, whether arriving or leaving. This spiritual practice is a reminder of our commitment to being disciples of Christ. As Romano Guardini reminds us, when we make the Sign of the Cross, this should be a purposeful gesture: "When we cross ourselves, let it be with a real sign of the cross. Instead of a small, cramped gesture that gives no notion of its meaning, let us make a large unhurried sign, from forehead to breast, from shoulder to shoulder, consciously feeling how it includes the whole of us, our thoughts, our attitudes, our body and soul, every part of us at once, how it consecrates and sanctifies us."[54] This year on Trinity Sunday, take time to reflect on why we make the Sign of the Cross and how we make this holiest of signs.

Trinitarian Symbols

Over the centuries, there have been different ways Christians have depicted the Holy Trinity. Not surprisingly, no symbol captures this infinite mystery clearly. For instance, St. Patrick's use of the shamrock to teach the people of Ireland about the Trinity is imperfect, as its three parts make up a single leaf but the Triune God is not "split" into parts. On this solemnity, it is a wonderful practice for Christian families to research the varied symbols used for the Trinity: the trefoil, the *fleur de lis*, or three fishes linked together, to name a few. The traditional diagram called the "Shield of the Trinity" can be especially helpful to children who are learning to understand the mystery that there are three distinct persons and each is God. Another image is that of God as Speaker, Word, and Breath: this captures the reality of the *logos*, the Incarnate Word, and the inseparable unity of the Trinity.

The Trisagion

The hymn to the thrice-holy Trinity (Holy, Holy, Holy) is a striking scriptural text found several times in the Church's liturgy, in both the East and the West: in the *Sanctus* at Mass, the *Te Deum*, and the reproaches during the adoration of the Cross on Good Friday (Isaiah 6:3, Revelation 4:8). Interestingly, this is the only text beside the *Kyrie eleison* to still be sung in Greek during the Roman Rite, as we hear on Good Friday: *Hagios O Theos, Hagios Athanatos, Hagios Ischyros, eleison hymas.* Many of us know this prayer from the Chaplet of Divine Mercy: "Holy God, Holy Strong One, Holy Immortal One have mercy on us." The Church promotes the use of this prayer in devotions as well. It is very fitting to recite on this solemnity, whether as part of another devotion or on its own. "The Trisagion is a pious exercise in which the faithful, united with the Angels, continually glorify God, the Holy, Powerful and Immortal One, while using expressions of praise drawn from Scripture and the Liturgy."[55]

The Athanasian Creed

Catholics are familiar with the Nicene Creed they proclaim every Sunday at Mass, as well as with the Apostles' Creed, which is prayed in the Rosary. A lesser known but important profession of faith is the Athanasian Creed, which is significant for its Christology, as it describes each Person of the Trinity as uncreated, limitless, eternal, and omnipotent. This text was prayed during the office of Prime on this feast day for many centuries. It is still a praiseworthy devotion to recite it on this day.

Singing Praise

In the Liturgy of the Hours, it is easy to note the regularity of the *Gloria Patri* (Glory be to the Father) at the end of each psalm or canticle, and its repetition throughout the day. This prayer is also repeated throughout the Rosary. Did you ever notice that it also forms the last verse of many classic hymns? In the tradition of hymnody, the final verse was always composed to be *doxological*, that is, giving glory to God and all three persons of the Trinity. Our voices raised in song, a symbol of our hearts united, are made for the purpose of giving praise to God. When we sing the doxology, or when we respond "Amen" to that great Eucharistic doxology at the Mass, we foreshadow that heavenly Jerusalem toward which we are journeying together.[56]

> Glory be to the Father, and to the Son, and to the Holy Spirit, as it was in the beginning, is now, and ever shall be, world without end. Amen.

The Most Holy Body and Blood of Christ
(*Corpus Christi*)

Thursday after Trinity Sunday, sixty days after Easter

Transferred to the Sunday after Trinity Sunday in the United States

Here beneath these signs are hidden
Priceless things to sense forbidden; / Signs, not things are all we see:
Blood is poured and flesh is broken, / Yet in either wondrous token
Christ entire we know to be.

–*Lauda Sion*, the Sequence for Corpus Christi

Catholic tradition has often referred to the Eucharist as "the bread of angels." While true in a certain sense, the Eucharist may more appropriately be called "the bread of God." For the sacrament of the Most Holy Body and Blood *comes from* God, *contains* God, and *transforms* into God those who eat it.

First, the Eucharist *comes from* God. He is the "divine baker and vintner," as it were. Man has had "food issues" from the beginning, ever since Adam and Eve ate of the forbidden tree. Since then, the descendants of Adam have sought to fill themselves on food that does not satisfy and slake their thirst on drink that does not quench. Part of the Father's "diet plan" for his children begins as the Chosen People journey through the desert. Responding to his people's wish for the food of their former days, the Lord provides manna: "In the evening quails came up and covered the camp; and in the morning dew lay round about the camp. And when the dew had gone up, there was on the face of the wilderness a fine, flake-like thing, fine as hoarfrost on the ground" (Exodus 16:13–14). The Lord also gave water to accompany them along their way to the Promised Land (see Exodus 17:6).

Later, with the coming of Christ, God gives us true bread and true drink—the very Body and Blood of his Son. The Father nourishes us with healthy food and drink by sending his Spirit "like the dewfall" upon mere bread and wine. As God's new People of God, the Church, we eat divine Bread and imbibe divine Drink on our journey to the "new Promised Land," heaven.

The Eucharist sustains us on our way because it truly is the Body, Blood, Soul, and Divinity of Jesus. Our belief that we are consuming God himself would be *un*-believable if God himself, in the person of Jesus, had not asserted it: "I am the living bread which came down from heaven … [M]y flesh is food indeed, and my blood is drink indeed" (John 6:51, 55; proclaimed in the Gospel of this solemnity during Year A). Jesus confirms his Eucharistic words at the Last Supper: "This is my body which is for you … This chalice is the new covenant in my blood" (1 Corinthians 11:24–25; the second reading at Mass during Year C; also Mark 14, the Gospel reading for Year B). The substance of the Eucharist—that which stands beneath it and fills it with reality—is God himself. "What could be more wonderful than this?" asks St. Thomas Aquinas (1225–1274) in the Office of Readings for the day.

Indeed, the Church expresses her wonder about the substance of the Eucharist in the Opening Prayer (Collect) of the Mass for this Solemnity. Unlike nearly every Collect throughout the liturgical year that is addressed to God the Father, the Opening Prayer on the Solemnity of Corpus Christi addresses the Eucharistic Christ himself:

"O God, who in this wonderful Sacrament have left us a memorial of your Passion, grant us, we pray, so to revere the sacred mysteries of your Body and Blood that we may always experience in ourselves the fruits of your redemption." But we hear this prayer regularly throughout the year as well. The Church prays this same text prior to Benediction with the Blessed Sacrament that concludes Eucharistic Adoration—she speaks directly to Christ, present before her.

Finally, we know that the Sacrament of the Eucharist is the food of God because of its remarkable effect upon those who receive it worthily. In short: we become what we eat—we become God. St. Thomas Aquinas not only contributed great philosophical and theological insights to our understanding of the Eucharist, but he also penned beautiful poetry celebrating the "sacrament of sacraments," including *Lauda Sion* ("Laud, O Sion"), *O Salutaris Hostia* ("O Saving Victim"), *Pange Lingua* ("Sing, my Tongue," a hymn the last two verses of which are sung as the *Tantum Ergo*), and *Sacris solemniis* (from which the term "bread of angels" comes). It is no wonder, then, that his words are heard throughout this solemnity.

The Office of Readings, for example, opens with one of his most remarkable lines: "Since it was the will of God's only-begotten Son that men should share in his divinity, he assumed our nature in order that by becoming man he might make men gods." Make men gods? But was this not the essence of the sin of our first parents—wanting to be gods? The central difference between their desire for divinization and ours depends wholly on who is doing the divinizing: Our first parents sought divinity according to their own designs, but our divinization comes from God's own will and power. And the Eucharist is one of his means to divinize us, to make us, as St. Thomas says, "gods."

Like St. Thomas, St. Augustine also saw the human and divine dynamic at work in the Eucharist. "I am the food of grown men," St. Augustine hears the Eucharistic Christ tell him. "Grow, and you shall feed upon me; nor shall you change me, like the food of your flesh, into yourself, but you shall be changed into me."[57] We really, truly become what we eat! As Pope Benedict XVI says, by the Eucharist we become blood relations, "consanguine," with Jesus: "The blood of Jesus is his love, in which divine life and human life have become one."[58]

Thus the "bread of angels" is first and foremost the "bread of God." It comes from him, it is filled with him, and it transforms in him all who receive it worthily. In this way, the Solemnity of Corpus Christi provides for us an opportunity to fill up our lives with God even as we recognize that we need no longer be fed up with the emptiness created by our fallen nature.

The Mass of Saint Gregory the Great, anonymous
(c. 1500) Groeningemuseum, Bruges

The theology of the Eucharist as sacrament of Christ's Body and Blood has been controversial from the moment he uttered the words "unless you eat the flesh of the Son of Man and drink his blood, you have no life in you," causing some of his disciples to abandon him (John 6:53, 66). In rebuking them, Christ says, "What if you see the Son of Man ascend to where he was before!" (John 6:62), claiming that his difficult words will be verified by a supernatural sign revealing his divinity. He uses a similar notion after telling the paralytic his sins were forgiven, telling the doubters that he would heal him to teach them that "the Son of man has authority on earth to forgive sins" (Matthew 9:1–7). Like so many of Christ's miracles in Scripture—and the long history of Eucharistic miracles that followed—suspensions of the physical laws were not mere spectacles, but evidence of his divinity and a remedy for disbelief. The Mass of Saint Gregory tells a similar story, becoming one of the most enduring renditions of a Eucharistic miracle in sacred art.

St. Gregory the Great reigned as pope from 590 to 604, and he is known for lending his name to Gregorian chant. But he was also a great scholar, writer, and liturgical reformer who appears frequently in the visual arts because of a dramatic Eucharistic miracle. Biographies dating to the eighth century tell the story of a "doubting matron" who baked the bread used at a Mass celebrated by Pope Gregory. When she came to receive the Eucharist, Gregory noted her skeptical smile. Asking her about it, he discovered that she could not believe that bread she baked in her own kitchen could become the Body of Christ. Concerned for her spiritual welfare, he prayed that she might believe, and suddenly her homemade bread became a strip of Christ's own flesh. Realizing the great miracle that happened before her eyes, she believed and wept in repentance. As with many pious stories, their retelling over the centuries causes transformations, and by the Middle Ages the story had changed considerably. The doubting woman came to be replaced by a doubting deacon, and rather than a small piece of flesh, Christ appears in his entirety. The story appeared in hundreds of versions throughout Europe in paintings, engravings, and even sculptures. And while the fundamental narrative remained fairly constant, particular renditions used a great variety of details.

Painted by an unknown Hispano-Flemish artist, this version shows Gregory—his office indicated by his triple tiara—kneeling in the center, his hands out in an expression of surprise as Christ appears before him, the deacon, and the subdeacon. One of the remarkable features of this rendition is its attention to liturgical detail. The figures' garments show a careful rendition of embroidery, even including attached pearls and gems. At the center of Gregory's vestment appears an embroidered shield adorned with a heart and

the two hands and feet of Christ. Known as the emblem of the Five Wounds of Christ, it grows from and reinforces the theme of the Eucharist as participation in Christ's Passion. The red silk cloth that hangs across the front of the altar, known as an antependium, shows its woven damask pattern, while the white altar cloth shows traces of having been folded. The illuminated letters of the altar missal are clearly evident, as is the missal's full-page depiction of the crucifixion, indicating that Gregory was saying the Eucharistic prayer when Christ appeared. The small screen attached to the rear of the altar, known as a reredos, shows three scenes from the Passion: the Carrying of the Cross on the left, the Descent from the Cross on the right, and presumably the Crucifixion itself immediately behind Christ.

Common to renditions of the Mass of Saint Gregory is the depiction of instruments of the Passion, shown here on the golden rear wall. Known as the *arma Christi*, the "weapons" of Christ used to defeat death and rescue humanity, they point out the irony that the armaments of Christ were implements used *against* him rather than *by* him. The Cross takes up the center place, while the top left shows thirty pieces of silver as the price of Judas' betrayal. Three dice appear on the top right, recalling the soldiers who gambled for Christ's seamless robe, which itself rests on the cross beam. The pillar of Christ's flagellation appears on the right, topped by the rooster that crowed three times at Peter's denial. Two brown rods with ropes tied to them—the instruments of the flagellation—appear to its left, with Veronica's veil above.

To the pillar's right appear the betraying kiss of Judas; the sword used by Peter to cut off the ear of the high priest's servant; the lantern carried by the soldiers who arrested Christ in the night; the pitcher and bowl used by Pilate to wash his hands of Christ's blood; and the hammer used to nail Christ to the Cross. To the left of the cross appear the ladder and pincers used to remove Christ's body from the cross; the lance which pierced his side; the rod with the sponge used to offer him a drink; the three nails of the crucifixion itself; and the hand that slapped his face. Several other faces appear, including the high priest Caiaphas on the far right, a man in a red hat spitting in Christ's face, and others who mocked or belittled him. Resting on the altar reredos near Christ's waist are two small jars containing gall and sour wine. Amidst the great detail, the Mass of Saint Gregory is a poetic representation of a historic event in the pope's life. But more importantly, it depicts a revelation of God and offers an engrossing opportunity for meditation on Christ's immense love. The facts of history prove merely the skeleton for an array of detail which at once confounds and intrigues the viewer, asking the worshipper to investigate, ask questions, and come to accept the profound offering of divine nourishment in the Body and Blood of Christ.

Celebrating Corpus Christi

The Second Vatican Council refers to the Eucharist as the "source and summit of Christian life."[59] Popular devotion and faith in the Eucharist led directly to the establishment of this solemnity. In 1264, Pope Urban IV extended this feast to the whole world as a result of the groundswell of ardent devotion to the Blessed Sacrament, as well as in response to controversies on the truth of the Real Presence. Eucharistic devotion reaches its pinnacle on this feast, which is brimming with expressions in the life of the faithful. Traditionally, the solemnity of Corpus Christi has been observed on the Thursday sixty days following Easter. However, in the dioceses of the United States and other places, it has been transferred to the following Sunday.

Eucharistic Processions

One of the most visible practices on this solemnity is a Eucharistic procession, in which the priest processes with a monstrance containing the Eucharist through and outside the church with incense, candles, a canopy, and honor guard, accompanied by singing and prayers. Typically, this procession takes place immediately following Mass, where the faithful journey with the Lord, and publicly proclaim faith in him, God-become-man. At the conclusion of the procession, a benediction is given with the Blessed Sacrament.

World Customs

In some parts of the world, Corpus Christi is celebrated as a civic festival day, with the streets of a town or city elaborately decorated for the Eucharistic procession. Throughout Europe and Latin America, this takes the form of "flower carpets," woven and arranged as a type of runner for the procession. In other places, these intricate designs are formed with colored sawdust, which takes many hours of preparation only to be trod on by the entire procession. Symbolically, it is a sacrifice akin to the jar of perfumed oil which was "wasted" on Jesus (see Matthew 26, Mark 14, Luke 7)—a gift of something beautiful and valuable offered for no other purpose than to give praise and honor to the Lord.

In Spain and Brazil, these floral carpets can reach more than half a mile in length. This festive atmosphere was captured by the Spanish composer Isaac Albeniz in his piano work *Iberia*, which depicts in the fourth movement the Corpus Christi festival in Seville, *Fête-dieu à Seville*. It calls to mind the marching bands that accompany the procession through the streets of the city and concludes with an interplay conjuring the sound of flamenco guitar with church bells ringing in the distance.

Forty Hours Devotion

On this weekend, many parishes celebrate the Forty Hours Devotion, which is a lengthy period of exposition of the Blessed Sacrament when people take turns keeping vigil and adoring the Lord. During this time, the faithful read Scripture, pray the Liturgy of the Hours, and engage in silent prayer and reflection before the Lord.

The number *forty* is highly significant in sacred time—the forty days of rain during the Flood, the forty years of Israel's wandering in the desert, and the Lord's forty days of fasting and prayer in the desert. The number forty also recalls Jesus' time in the tomb from his burial to his resurrection.

Hymns for the Home

St. Thomas Aquinas wrote several pieces of liturgical poetry specifically for the feast of Corpus Christi: the *Pange Lingua* (which is often sung during the transfer of the Blessed Sacrament on Holy Thursday) and its final verse, *Tantum Ergo*, which is traditionally sung at Benediction. He also wrote the sequence *Lauda Sion*, which contains the well-known *Panis Angelicus*. On this day, whether you hear these hymns at Mass or not, pray or even sing these beautiful pieces in your home to deepen your family's devotion to the Holy Eucharist.

As Pope Benedict XVI writes in *Sacramentum Caritatis*, "the Eucharist is at the root of every form of holiness, and each of us is called to the fullness of life in the Holy Spirit … holiness has always found its center in the Sacrament of the Eucharist."[60]

Eucharistic Miracles and the Modern Age

One of the beautiful stories about this feast day is the miracle of Orvieto. In the thirteenth century, a German priest who had doubts about the Real Presence of Christ in the Eucharist came to visit Italy. As he celebrated Mass, during the consecration he saw a drop of blood fall from the host into the chalice. He immediately went to visit the pope, who was in Orvieto, and brought the host to him. As a result, the Cathedral of Orvieto was erected as a shrine to this Eucharistic miracle.[61]

In modern times, stories of Eucharistic miracles are easily accessible to us. On Corpus Christi, children, especially teenagers, should learn about Blessed Carlo Acutis. He was a computer whiz who used the Internet to tell the stories of Eucharistic miracles, even while battling leukemia as a teenager. Storytelling, especially of the lives of the saints who were models of Eucharistic devotion, is a wonderful tradition to have as a family.

The Most Sacred Heart of Jesus

The Friday that follows the second Sunday after Pentecost

The expression "poured out" appears time and again in the Church's liturgical texts during solemnities. For example, the Opening Prayer for Mass during the Day at Pentecost asks the Father to "*pour out* the gifts of the Holy Spirit across the face of the earth." In the second reading for the solemnity of the Most Holy Trinity, St. Paul tell us that "the love of God has been *poured out* into our hearts through the Holy Spirit" (Romans 5:5). As St. Thomas Aquinas' *Lauda Sion*, from the solemnity of *Corpus Christi*, teaches us, "Blood is poured and flesh is broken / Yet in either wondrous token / Christ entire we know to be." The solemnity of the Sacred Heart of Jesus continues this current of thought, and it shows us the source of God's gracious gifts—the opened heart of the Redeemer upon the Cross.

On this solemnity, St. John the Evangelist takes us back to this source: "One of the soldiers pierced his side with a spear, and at once there came out blood and water" (John 19:34; Gospel reading for Year B). Recall that the entire drama on Calvary—including the centurion's stab—is *re-presented* on the altar of sacrifice. And just as that moment in time is about to come before us on the altar, the Church says similarly in her Preface text for the day, "raised up high on the Cross, he gave himself up for us with a wonderful love and poured out blood and water from his pierced side, the wellspring of the Church's sacraments." For this reason—Jesus opening the wellspring of his heart—our thirsty souls are able to drink in the great graces about to pour forth. As St. Bonaventure (1221–1274) writes, "Press your lips to the fountain … and draw water from the wells of your Savior; for this is the spring flowing out of the middle of paradise, dividing into four rivers, inundating devout hearts, watering the whole earth and making it fertile" (from the day's Office of Readings). In short, the Solemnity of the Sacred Heart of Jesus opens up for us the source of our life and heartsick longing.

Truly, the exact object of this solemnity is the very heart of Jesus, which is itself the symbol of God's love for us. As the Solemnity of Christmas reveals the birth of Jesus, the Solemnity of Mary, Mother of God, honors the Blessed Mother, or the Solemnity of Saints Peter and Paul honors these apostles, so the solemnity of the Sacred Heart of Jesus brings us into the opened heart of the Redeemer and surrounds us with divine love.

The heart of the Trinity first poured itself out in a loving act at creation. Indeed, as St. John teaches us, "God is love" (1 John 4:16). Even after mankind rejected this love, God's love for us continues. "When Israel was a child I loved him, and out of Egypt I called my son … [M]y compassion grows warm and tender" (Hosea 11:1, 8; the first reading for Mass in Year B). At Jesus' Incarnation, the same love that gave us life and sustained our being poured itself out so that we might enjoy eternal life and share in the being of God himself. "For God so loved the world that he gave his only-begotten Son, that whoever believes in him should not perish but have eternal life" (John 3:16). And this love of God, this love who *is* God, is the object of our devotion to the heart of Christ: As Pope Pius XII explains, the devotion to the "infinite love of God for the human race … demands of us a complete and unreserved determination to devote and consecrate ourselves to the love of the divine Redeemer, whose wounded heart is its living token and symbol" (*Haurietis Aquas*, 20, 6).

How, then, do we respond? How do we love *love*? St. Margaret Mary Alacoque (1647–1690) was not the first Christian to respond with her heart to the love of God, but she did receive inspiration from Christ himself to honor him on each First Friday of every month. Others make holy hours in honor of his love. The Enthronement of the Sacred Heart of Jesus, where an image or statue of Christ and his Sacred Heart is solemnly erected in the home, school, or office, becomes a true beating heart in the midst of the day. For others still, the Morning Offering lifts up our prayers, works, joys, and sufferings along with the Eucharist "for all the intentions of your Sacred Heart."

The attentive ear will also find direction from the Mass's prayers and texts on this day about how to respond with devotion to the Heart of God. The psalm between the readings, for example, employs Psalm 23 and these verses: "Even though I walk through the valley of the shadow of death / I fear no evil / for you are with me / your rod and your staff / they comfort me" (Psalm 23:4): so be fearless and courageous! The Preface asks of the Father that, "won over to the open heart of the Savior, all might draw water joyfully from the springs of salvation": let us be joyful! Let us pour that joy out to share with others. For, as the Prayer after Communion proclaims: "May this sacrament of charity, O Lord, make us fervent with the fire of holy love, so that, drawn always to your Son, we may learn to see him in our neighbor."

The solemnity of the Sacred Heart celebrates the great gift of divine love in the form of Christ's human heart. It also calls us to join our hearts with his and radiate divine love to all in our midst. O Sacred Heart of Jesus: have mercy on us!

The *Sacred Heart of Jesus*, central panel of a three-part mural, by Leonard Porter
(2004) Cathedral of St. Joseph, Sioux Falls, South Dakota

In 2001, New York painter Leonard Porter was offered a rare opportunity. Together with architects who specialized in classical architecture, Porter was asked to paint a church mural of Renaissance proportions. Over seven feet high and twenty feet wide, it features more than two dozen figures, an idealized landscape, secondary narratives, and multiple symbolic still life tableaux. While traditional Catholic painting would see a revival over the next twenty years, in 2001, this was a groundbreaking image. Porter was a pioneer of classical narrative painting, largely shunned both by the art world and liturgical establishment since the advent of Modernism in the mid-twentieth century. A self-taught classicist, Porter used his radically traditional method and layered narratives to make the centerpiece of a Blessed Sacrament chapel dedicated to the Sacred Heart of Jesus. The result was an image outside of time yet believably corporeal, with both an active stillness and heavenly calm centered on both the Real Presence and Christ's loving heart.

Unlike most devotional images, which show Christ or a saint isolated from their surroundings, Porter's image shows Christ in his glory, adored by angels and saints in a heavenly setting. He sits on a throne atop a large pedestal in the form of a tomb, marking that he is the victor over death, reigning in glory after the Resurrection. His exposed torso indicates his clear and evident humanity, still showing the wounds of his passion and his Sacred Heart. The arms of his throne, made of marble, gold, and bronze, support two small globes representing Christ's lordship over both heaven and earth. On the viewer's left appears the terrestrial sphere, centered on Jerusalem, the place of Christ's salvific work. On the right, the globe appears as the night sky, the constellations arranged as they appeared in the sky over Bethlehem at the birth of Christ. Over each shoulder appear two golden winged figures, each holding emblems of victory: a crown and the palm branch of martyrdom.

At the feet of Jesus appears a red rectangle containing the letters IHS, a traditional monogram for Christ, which is a contraction of the name Jesus. A torn pomegranate appears near Christ's right foot, referring primarily to Christ's Sacred Heart, since the shape resembles a human heart and its interior structure is made up of chambers filled with blood-red juice. But the pomegranate also symbolizes the unity of the Church, since its thick rind provides protection for many individual members inside. It also recalls the Resurrection, since when burst open, like Christ's tomb, its life is available for all the world.

Standing below Christ are six biblical saints, including Joseph, the Virgin Mary, Peter, Paul, John the Evangelist, and John the Baptist. Peeking through in the landscape between the tomb and the saints appear many small classical temples, indicating the worship and architecture of the ancient world now brought to Christian perfection. Similarly, Porter places a small rendition of the actual cathedral in which this mural sits into the landscape, bending concepts of time to indicate the timelessness of God's providence. In a *tour de force* move, he places the cathedral in the background so it appears to sit in the outstretched hands of St. Joseph, allowing him to exercise his intercessory role as patron, both supporting the cathedral and offering it to Christ.

On the steps of the tomb appear several still life compositions that refer to the Paschal Mystery. A chalice appears on the top step, a clear reference to the Eucharist. The step below shows three containers, each of different appearance, containing the gold, frankincense, and myrrh brought to the Christ child by the Magi. Gold, indicated by the gem-covered chest, signified Christ's kingship, while incense, shown in an Egyptian-styled canopic jar used in pharaohs' tombs, was offered in worship to God, indicating Jesus' divinity. The red and black jar contains myrrh, a sweet-smelling perfume used to anoint bodies before burial, and therefore an indication of Christ's passion. In Porter's creative genius, he took inspiration from Greek vase painting to show on the jar's decoration—less than two inches high—a funeral procession, thereby giving layers of meaning to a seemingly simple object.

On the ground level, another grouping of Christological images appears. Placed next to the hammer used to drive the nails through Christ's hands and feet, the skull refers to Golgotha, the place of the Crucifixion, whose name literally means "place of the skull." Coins and dice refer to the soldiers who gambled for Christ's garment, with the holly branch, too, recalling the Passion of Christ because of its blood-red berries and prickly leaves that recall the crown of thorns. A ribbon-like banner winds through the scene, displaying in Greek, Hebrew, and Latin the name fixed atop Christ's cross—Jesus of Nazareth, King of the Jews. Lastly, a colorful, red-faced bird sits atop it all: the European Goldfinch. Unlike the bright yellow American Goldfinch, the European variety has bright red feathers around its face. The Christian legend tells that at the Crucifixion, a passing goldfinch was moved to compassion for Christ. Since it was accustomed to eating seeds from prickly thistles, it attempted to remove the thorns from Christ's head, and was forever stained with the blood of Christ. Moreover, the bird is a sign of resurrection, since medieval legends told that the childhood playmates of Jesus would bring him sculpted birds made of clay, and he would bring them to life, much as God breathed life into Adam, who was made from the dust of the earth.

Though painted in the twenty-first century, Porter's mural does what all great Christian murals do: reveal the truth of God's salvific plan as lived out in creation, human culture, signs of the Covenant, and signs taken up by Christ. It allows the worshippers of today to enter the same reality of Christ's mercy with angels and saints, bending time and space to experience heaven on earth.

Celebrating the Solemnity of the Sacred Heart

The Vision of the Heart of Jesus of St. Margaret Mary Alacoque,
Unknown Artist

As Blessed Columba Marmion says, "Love explains all the mysteries of Jesus; the faith that we ought to have in the fullness of this love; the Church sets it before us as the object of worship in the Feast of the Sacred Heart."[62] Out of love for our Lord, Christians have long had a devotion in a particular way to the Sacred Heart of Jesus, which in Christian iconography is depicted for us, as "the wound in the Heart symbolized the wound of love."[63] In 1671, St. Margaret Mary Alacoque entered the Daughters of the Visitation founded by St. Francis de Sales and St. Jane Frances de Chantal. Between 1673 and 1675, she had visions of our Lord in which he spoke to her of the overwhelming love of his divine Heart. On the feast of St. John, Jesus allowed Margaret Mary to rest her head upon his Heart, and then revealed to her the depths of his love. He made specific requests to her, including the establishment of this feast day.

As Pope Leo XIII writes about this encounter, "There is in the Sacred Heart a symbol and a sensible image of the infinite love of Jesus Christ which moves us to love one another."[64] Devotion to the Sacred Heart of Jesus focuses on receiving this love of Christ and giving it back to him in thanksgiving.

First Fridays

The practice of attending Mass on the first Friday of each month is one of the specific requests of our Lord to show devotion to his Sacred Heart. During one of his apparitions to St. Margaret Mary, Jesus asked for frequent communion, including communion on the first Friday of every month. The Lord promises that those who receive communion on nine first Fridays will not die without the chance to repent of their sins.

Act of Reparation

The third request Our Lord gave to St. Margaret Mary was for a solemn act of reparation for all offenses made against him in the Blessed Sacrament. On this solemnity, we can gain a plenary indulgence by making an act of reparation to the Sacred Heart. This must be publicly recited in a church, in a religious community, or within a family, under the usual conditions for indulgences. This practice was promoted for all the faithful by Pius XI in his 1928 encyclical *Miserentissimus Redemptor*. The act of reparation consists of recognizing one's own sinfulness, a readiness to make amends for one's sins and atonement for others' sins against Jesus, offer reparations, and recommit oneself to a life of virtue.

Prayer for Priests

The month of June is dedicated to the Sacred Heart, which is the solemnity for the world day of prayer for priests. In his general audience of June 17, 2020, Pope Francis said, "I invite everyone to look to that heart and imitate its most authentic sentiments. Pray for all Priests and for my Petrine Ministry, so that all pastoral actions may bear the imprint of the love that Christ bears for each human being." In particular, pray for the priests who baptized you, gave you first Holy Communion, celebrated your wedding, heard your most recent confession—even if you cannot recall all their names!—as

well as for your pastor and the bishop of your diocese. Pray also for the perseverance of priests and those in priestly formation. A novena to the Sacred Heart begins nine days before this feast and provides the opportunity to remember in prayer all of the priests who led us closer to Christ.

Sacred Heart Fires

One tradition in the South Tyrol region of Italy is for the hills and mountains to be illuminated with fires in the shape of crosses and hearts. This recalls a promise the Tyroleans made in 1796, when they fought against oppression from outside forces. They pledged eternal allegiance to the Sacred Heart and defeated the French troops. Later, they fought off an attack from Bavaria. Every year, they renew this pledge on this solemnity. While these midsummer fires have their origin in St. John's fires (see the Nativity of St. John the Baptist), in this region they came to signify the people's pledge to the Sacred Heart. Perhaps you can host a Sacred Heart fire in your own backyard, along with your other devotions of this day, such as a prayer for priests.

Enthronement in the Home

Among his twelve promises to St. Margaret Mary, Jesus said that he would bless every place where the image of his Sacred Heart was honored. Many Catholic families have taken up the practice of enthronement, which is placing images of the Sacred Heart of Jesus and the Immaculate Heart of Mary in a prominent place in the home where they can be honored. During this enthronement, the family consecrates itself to the Sacred Heart.

When Pope Leo XIII consecrated the world to the Sacred Heart, he proclaimed that the flames of Our Lord's heart are an image of his love.[65] Enthronement of these images in the home is a practice that proclaims this love to the world and deepens the love of Christ radiating from the family. As Blessed Columba Marmion writes, "Everything that the created love accomplishes is in union with the uncreated love, and on account of it; Christ's Heart draws its human kindness from the Divine ocean."[66]

The Nativity of St. John the Baptist

June 24

This child, born to us, is greater than any prophet; the Savior said of him:
There is no man born of women greater than John the Baptist.

–Marian antiphon for Evening Prayer II

Everybody loves a birthday party. In the sacrament of Baptism, Christians celebrate their birth from the womb of the Church into the new life of grace. Martyrs and saints celebrate another sort of birthday when, after laying down their earthly life for Christ, they enter eternal life in heaven. Interestingly, though, the Church does not typically celebrate the actual birthdays of saints—with the exceptions of the Blessed Virgin Mary and John the Baptist.

In the Office of Readings for this solemnity, St. Augustine remarks, "The Church observes the birth of John as a hallowed event. We have no such commemoration for any other fathers; but it is significant that we celebrate the birthdays of John and of Jesus. This day cannot be passed by." But as we stop to reflect on this solemn birthday, the Church directs our attention to the many days leading up to John's nativity. Indeed, the oft-mentioned "womb" from the day's liturgies that formed John had been prepared for centuries prior to his birth.

As with his cousin Jesus, John did not come into the world without preparation or context. The prophet Isaiah resembles John nearly seven hundred years prior to his birth. We hear at the Mass during the day that the Lord "formed me from the womb to be his servant, to bring Jacob back to him" (Isaiah 49:5). Similar verses from the prophet Jeremiah are read at the Vigil Mass and at the Office of Readings: "Before I formed you in the womb I knew you, and before you were born I consecrated you" (Jeremiah 1:5). Like Isaiah and Jeremiah before him, John's nativity involved a good deal of divine "prenatal" care.

The preparation leading to John's birth also resembles the Old Testament figures of Isaac and Samuel—or, rather, his parents are much like theirs. Isaac was born to Abraham and Sarah when they were "advanced in age" and beyond normal childbearing years (see Genesis 18:11). Similarly, Samuel's mother, Hannah, was childless and apparently infertile. After praying to the Lord at the Temple, though, God granted her a son (see 1 Samuel 1:1–20). John's parents, Zechariah and Elizabeth, were similarly childless, "because Elizabeth was barren, and both were advanced in years" (Luke 1:7). The age and infertility of John's parents not only shows how miraculous was his birth ("I praise you, for I am wonderfully made," the psalm response for the Mass during the day says), but also that he is the culmination and completion of the Old Testament. As St. Augustine remarks in the Office of Readings, John "represents times past and is the herald of the new era to come. As a representative of the past, he is born of aged parents; as a herald of the new era, he is declared to be a prophet while still in his mother's womb."

In addition to Old Testament prophets and parents preparing the way for John—who will, in turn, "prepare the way of the Lord" (Matthew 3:3, Mark 1:3)—nature itself shines a light on John and his divine cousin to help us appreciate their births. The Church also celebrates John's and Jesus' conceptions on September 23 and March 25, respectively, and their births on June 24 and December 25. These four dates approximate the beginning of our earth's seasons: the Nativity of St. John is celebrated near the time of the summer solstice and earth's longest day on (or around) June 21 in the northern hemisphere, while his conception is celebrated near the time of the autumnal equinox on September 21. Likewise, Christmas is celebrated near the time of the winter solstice on December 21; and the Annunciation is celebrated near the time of the vernal equinox around March 21. Thus, the sun, moon, and earth form a part of that "womb" that weaves meaning into the life and mission of John the Baptist: "I must decrease," says the forerunner born just as the earth's days grow shorter, so that "he may increase," John says of Christ, born as the earth's "light of the world" as our days begin to lengthen.

In fact, the significance of their births' proximity to the longest and shortest days of the year plays out elsewhere. Many depictions of St. John the Baptist in his prime find him pointing to Christ, saying in gesture, "Behold, the Lamb of God!" He similarly directs our attention to Christ when proclaiming, "He is mightier than I" (see Luke 3:16). His humility also shows itself when, asked by Christ for baptism, "John would have prevented him, saying, 'I need to be baptized by you, and do you come to me?'" (Matthew 3:14). Once again, St. Augustine makes this point clear in the day's Office of Readings: "John was a voice that lasted only for a time; Christ, the Word in the beginning, is eternal." In short, St. John's mission directs us away from himself and toward Christ.

Elizabeth's womb formed a prophet with the stature of Isaiah and Jeremiah. With the help of God, she conceived St. John in miraculous and divine fashion. In bearing her son, Elizabeth brought to conclusion the old age of the promises and began a new day, giving birth to the forerunner of the Dawn. Is it any wonder that Zechariah, on seeing such a son, would utter at his birth the great proclamation which the Church even today makes a part of her Morning Prayer: "Blessed be the Lord, the God of Israel, for he has visited and brought redemption to his people … And you, child, will be called prophet of the Most High, for you will go before the Lord to prepare his ways, to give his people knowledge of salvation through the forgiveness of their sins" (Luke 1:68, 76–79).

St. John the Baptist was more than a "warm-up act" for the Lord—he was a man after Christ's heart, knowing from the moment he leapt in Elizabeth's womb that the Savior of the world had come to earth. And John's birth was in its own way a supernatural event in salvation history. In celebrating the Solemnity of the Nativity of St. John the Baptist, the entire Church draws back the curtain on the new life which Christ's own birth brings.

The Birth and Naming of John the Baptist, from the Saint John Altarpiece, by Rogier Van der Weyden (c. 1454), Gemäldegalerie, Berlin

Ut queant laxis, a traditional hymn to St. John the Baptist, includes the verse "coming from heaven, Gabriel the angel told your father of your coming birthday, named you and gave him details of your actions, foretelling greatness." Though the line is addressed to John, it speaks about his father, Zechariah, as told in the first chapter of the Gospel of Luke. Zechariah and his wife Elizabeth, though righteous, were elderly and childless. Yet the angel Gabriel appears to him in the Temple and tells him that his wife would bear a son named John who would be filled with the Holy Spirit "even from his mother's womb" (Luke 1:15). Because he did not believe this possible, Zechariah was made mute, generating great interest among the local people about this coming child and the meaning of his birth. To this day the Church remembers John's nativity liturgically, the only birthday other than those of Christ and the Virgin found in the Church's universal calendar, because his birth was intricately bound up with the nativity of the Savior, for whom John was known as "the Precursor."

Rogier van der Weyden's image of the Baptist's birth forms the left section of a three-part painting known as the *Saint John Triptych*. Historians have placed him in the "early Netherlandish" tradition, characterized by attention to realistic detail within a poetic form of narrative and representation. Commissioned for a Carthusian monastery, the painting presents the narrative of the Precursor's birth. But more importantly, it invites contemplation on the meaning of his role in God's plan of salvation through theologically informed departures from the biblical story and numerous secondary details.[67] The story of the Baptist's actual birth appears in the middle ground, with Elizabeth in her richly furnished bed, attended by a servant. Visitors enter through a small door in the background, consonant with the note that "her neighbors and kinsfolk heard that the Lord had shown great mercy to her, and they rejoiced with her" (Luke 1:58). The largest figures—the Virgin and Zechariah—appear in front of the great arch, which historians have interpreted as a choice by van der Weyden to indicate that the ideas presented there are not merely historical but continued living realities.

Zechariah appears on the right, eyes fixed on the Virgin. Luke's Gospel relates that family members and neighbors wanted to name the child Zechariah after his father, but Elizabeth declared that he would be named John. Seeking his input, Zechariah was given a pen and tablet, and, fulfilling the request of the angel, wrote, "His name is John." Suddenly able to speak, he proclaimed his famous Canticle, foretelling that his son would be "called the prophet of the Most High" and "go before the Lord to prepare his way" (Luke 1:76).

Accordingly, van der Weyden portrayed Zechariah with pen in hand. But in a departure from Scripture, van der Weyden shows the infant John in the arms of the Virgin, even though Luke wrote she had already left for home (Luke 1:56).

To explain this departure from Scripture, it is important to note that the scene is not meant to be a literal account, but rather an exposition of its theological importance: the Baptist is a bridge figure who completes the work of the Old Testament prophets and ushers in the new age of Christian revelation. While previous prophets could only speak of Christ through metaphors, John the Baptist pointed directly to the person of Christ and said, "Behold the Lamb of God who takes away the sins of the world!" (John 1:29). Moreover, he had already done this from within his mother's womb at the Visitation of Mary and Elizabeth, leaping in joy under the inspiration of the Holy Spirit. John, then, was chosen to "give" Christ to the nascent Church, represented in the painting by the figure of the Virgin. Mary is widely known as one who typifies the Church because through her, Christ was given to the world. By "giving" John to the Virgin, Zechariah thereby fulfills his mission to cooperate with the angel Gabriel and usher in the coming of the Messiah. Van der Weyden highlights the Christological and Mariological reading of the Baptist's birth in six canopied carvings, called archivolts, appearing in the arch overhead. Running counterclockwise from the left, the first scene shows the appearance of Gabriel to Zechariah, and the next, Zechariah being struck speechless. The scenes then proceed to the Marriage of the Virgin, the Annunciation to Mary, the Visitation of Mary and Elizabeth, and finally the Nativity of Christ, marking the lineage from Zechariah to Christ.

As John was the precursor to Christ, so Zechariah was a precursor to John, and the complex narrative shows a poetic fittingness that characterizes salvation history. Zechariah had lost his voice, yet John became the voice proclaiming Christ, who himself was the voice of God Incarnate. And the Virgin features prominently in it all. As Saint Augustine noted, John was born in a seemingly impossible situation: to a woman past childbearing age. Similarly, Christ's conception seemed impossible as well: he was born of a virgin. John was conceived by a father who did not believe, yet Christ was born of a mother who accepted the will of God. Because he was the last of the old prophets, John was born of an elderly couple, yet as the herald of the new, he proclaimed Christ's coming even from the womb.[68] So van der Weyden's painting presents more than the story of John the Baptist alone but reveals, as did the Baptist himself, his place in God's plan of salvation.

Celebrating the Nativity of St. John the Baptist

As early as the year 506, the Nativity of St. John the Baptist was celebrated with special festivity, as a day free of servile work and with the obligation to attend Mass. In some places, a fourteen-day fast preceded this feast. Many churches have dedicated their baptisteries to John the Baptist, and they often have a statue or image of him nearby. Traditionally, one of the three Masses of the day could be celebrated *ad fontem*—that is, at the baptistery. John the Baptist is the patron saint of those condemned to death, especially those condemned as a result of their witness to the faith.

The celebration of John's birth on this date is somewhat confusing, as we wonder why it is not June 25 to correspond with six months preceding the date of Christmas. Actually, both feasts fall on the eighth day prior to the beginning of the next month, in agreement with Luke 1:36.[69] Other feast days for this great saint have been celebrated in the history of the Church, such as the feast of his conception (September 23), which is still observed in the Byzantine tradition.

St. John's Fires

On hilltops and mountains around Europe, fires have been lit on the eve of this feast in a custom originating from pre-Christian times. As a celebration of the return of summer, these fires burned as a symbol of the return of warmth from Norway to Spain. The practice of lighting and gathering around fires in villages welcomed the "saint of summer" in a Christianized ritual that has been documented since the sixth century. Parishes, communities, and families gather around bonfires to celebrate this feast day. The Roman Ritual contains a blessing of a fire specifically for the eve of the feast of St. John the Baptist, as John's mission was to witness to the light (see John 1:7).

A common question Catholics have is about what to do with blessed objects that are broken or can no longer be used, for instance, a rosary. As the blessed object cannot simply be thrown out, it needs to be returned to the earth (i.e., buried) or burned. Some are shocked to learn that we would burn blessed items, but it is important to remember that we burn the previous year's blessed palms to make ashes for Ash Wednesday, and we also burn "old" holy oils. Some parishes ask parishioners to bring in their broken or unusable sacramental objects on this solemnity, so that they can be properly disposed of in the blessed fire. The Church's *Directory on Popular Piety* commends the custom of blessing bonfires on this day: "The Church blesses such fires, praying God that the faithful may overcome the darkness of the world and reach the 'indefectible light' of God."[70] Often, the community gathering at the bonfire is accompanied by traditional foods, singing, and folk dancing.

Singing Around the Fire

A great piece of Catholic trivia surrounds the origin of the notes of the musical scale. Many of us are familiar with the syllables *do, re, mi, fa, sol, la, ti, do* from music class in elementary school or from the song from a certain popular musical. Did you know that these syllables actually originated in music from this feast day? The hymn for Vespers for the Nativity of St. John the Baptist in Latin is:

Ut queant laxis resonare fibris
Mira gestorum famuli tuorum,
Solve polluti labii reatum,
Sancte Joannes.

"So that your servants may sing at the top of their voices the wonders of your acts, and absolve the fault from their stained lips, St. John."

Each phrase of the hymn begins one step higher. If you are familiar with a piano keyboard, the word *ut* would be on C, *resonare* would start on D, *mira* on E, etc. for each of the first six notes. A monk named Guido of Arezzo who lived in the early eleventh century excerpted the first syllable of each phrase in Latin to use as a memory aid in teaching the ascending musical scale. This is how we end up with these solmization syllables (or "*solfège*") that we know today. The original first syllable "*ut*" was later changed to "*do*" because "*do*" produces a more beautiful choral sound when sung. This memory aid helped singers more easily remember the relationship between musical pitches and made it simpler to sightread new music once notation systems were more fully developed. Be sure to thank and pray for your school music teacher on this day, especially if you remember your *do-re-mi*.

Most fitting in the Northern Hemisphere: the light from the Sun gradually decreases following the summer solstice (proximate to this feast day). After the Nativity of the Lord, the light from the Sun gradually increases. These natural sacramental signs correspond with the Scriptures, assisting us in contemplating the beauty of the order of creation. The movement of the celestial bodies reflects the logical design of God, foreshadowing the Gospel: "I might decrease so that he may increase" (John 3:30).

Saints Peter and Paul, Apostles

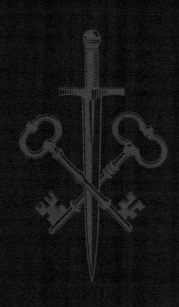

June 29

For by your providence
the blessed Apostles Peter and Paul bring us joy:
Peter, foremost in confessing the faith,
Paul, its outstanding preacher,
Peter, who established the early Church
from the remnant of Israel,
Paul, master and teacher of the Gentiles that you call.

–Preface from the Mass for this solemnity

Saints Peter and Paul were the master builders who executed the plans of the divine architect, Jesus. Yet the two men could not have been more different. St. Peter was a hardscrabble fisherman from Galilee. Despite his human limitations and failures, he became the Rock that supports the Church, shedding his blood by crucifixion in Rome. St. Paul, on the other hand, came from Tarsus in modern-day Turkey, where his family were tentmakers. Paul was well-educated, a fervent Pharisee, and an early persecutor of Christians before meeting the Lord on the road to Damascus and becoming his "apostle to the Gentiles." Like Peter, he too died in Rome under the emperor Nero. As a Roman citizen, however, he could not be crucified; so he was beheaded.

Despite their differences, and because of their common mission for Christ, Peter and Paul combined to form a solid foundation for the Church. As St. Augustine notes in this solemnity's Office of Readings, "Both apostles share the same feast day, for these two were one; and even though they suffered on different days, they were as one. Peter went first, and Paul followed. And so we celebrate this day made holy for us by the apostles' blood."

Traditionally, these "blood brothers" were celebrated on different days on the liturgical calendar. In fact, each still has a feast day of his own, apart from the current solemnity: the conversion of St. Paul on January 25 and the Chair of St. Peter on February 22. In the early centuries, June 29 saw the celebration of two Masses—one in commemoration of St. Peter took place where his great basilica now stands, and another Mass in honor of St. Paul at his eponymous basilica "outside the walls" in Rome. Due to the distance between these basilicas and the time it took to travel between them, however, St. Paul's feast came to be observed a day later than St. Peter's, on June 30. Today, their collaborative role in the Church's foundation is marked on this June 29 solemnity.

Since bishops are the successors of the apostles, this solemnity is particularly appropriate to celebrate the ordination of bishops. We might consider the parallel between these first bishops and their flocks with those of today. Peter went through a trial of trust and denied Christ, and Paul went so far as to kill Christ's followers. Their subjects were quick to deny the faith they were given: "O foolish Galatians! Who has bewitched you?" (Galatians 3:1). Bishops and faithful must continue to encourage and pray for each other. As a bishop himself, St. Augustine exhorts us, "Let us embrace what they believed, their life, their labors, their sufferings, their preaching and their confession of faith."

The ultimate "confession of faith" of Peter and Paul comes by shedding their blood. The entrance antiphon for Mass during the day of their solemnity focuses our minds on this mystery in these words: "These are the ones who, living in the flesh, planted the Church with their blood; they drank the chalice of the Lord and became the friends of God."

In addition to the Church's liturgy keeping their martyrdom before us on this day, it also emphasizes Peter's profession and Paul's teaching. During Christ's Passion, Peter denied Christ three times: "I do not know the man." During the days of Christ's presence to the apostles after his resurrection, Peter confessed Christ three times: "Yes, Lord; you know that I love you." This passage recalling Peter's confession (John 21:15–19) is read at the Vigil Mass for the Solemnity and exemplifies not only Christ's patience and love for his followers, but how each of us is constantly called to return to Christ after betraying him by sin. In the Gospel reading for the Mass during the day, we hear another of Peter's professions: "You are the Christ, the Son of the living God" (Matthew 16:16). Confirming his testimony, Jesus tells him: "You are Peter, and on this rock I will build my Church" (Matthew 16:18). Peter's blood, along with his confession, forms the solid rock upon which the Church rises. Even Paul calls Peter "Cephas," or "Rock" (Galatians 1:18, heard in the second reading at the Vigil Mass, as well as in the Office of Readings).

If Peter's mission emphasized professing Christ to his fellow Jews, the Chosen People, Paul's announcement was to the Gentiles. God "was pleased to reveal his Son to me, in order that I might preach him among the Gentiles" (Galatians 1:16), we hear in Paul's letter to the Galatians at the Vigil Mass. The next day the Church reads a similar sentiment from Paul's second letter to another bishop, St. Timothy: "But the Lord stood by me and gave me strength to proclaim the word fully, that all the Gentiles might hear it" (2 Timothy 4:17). Paul's writings constitute a majority of the New Testament texts. His preaching speaks with his blood of the saving power of God available to all in the Church.

The faith in Christ that sustains us today rests upon the foundations of the apostles: on their blood, in their confession, by their teaching. Without their place in the history of salvation—the place that the Church remembers with the present Solemnity—our faith would have crumbled long ago. The solemn blessing today is a fitting way to keep our faith alive every day: "by the keys of St. Peter and the words of St Paul, and by the support of their intercession, [may God] bring us happily to that homeland that Peter attained on a cross and Paul by the blade of a sword."

ΠΕΤΡ · S· PAVLVS·

Icon of the Embrace of the Apostles Peter and Paul by Angelos Akotantos
(c. 1436–1450) The Ashmolean Museum of Art and Archaeology, Oxford

To many Catholics of the Roman rite, the icons of the East can appear both intriguing and somewhat off-putting. On the one hand, their mystical quality is obvious, yet their departure from literal reality and seemingly inexpressive detachment can make them seem lifeless and emotionally unsatisfying. In part this reaction comes from the Western Church's inheritance of Aristotle and his "bottom up" approach to understanding the truth of things, in which creation and experience lead one up to God. But the Christian East remains strongly marked by the inheritance of Plato, whose philosophy is often described as "top down," in which the perfection of heaven becomes known in the matter of the world. While an embrace between Saints Peter and Paul might be portrayed in the West with evident emotion and realistic depiction of bodies and gestures, an iconic representation emphasizes the heavenly and transfigured quality of their feelings, bodies, poses, and even clothing. So Angelos Akotantos, one of the most important Greek iconographers of the fifteenth century, revealed the theological reality of two saints in an iconic way: both martyrs, both Jews, one an apostle to the Gentiles, come together in a fraternal kiss representing the unity of the Church.

Icons are frequently associated with Orthodox Churches, and interestingly, the term "orthodox" in this case refers in part to right theology about icons. In 726, Byzantine Emperor Leo III declared all sacred images to be idols and ordered their destruction. Decades of theological and political fighting followed, settled in part by the Council of Nicaea in 787, which defined the proper role and use of sacred images. A second period of iconoclasm, which literally means "icon breaking," began in the ninth century, finally ending in 842 with the permanent acceptance of visual images. In celebration, the Byzantine Church added a new feast to its calendar in honor of icons, known as the "Feast of the Triumph of Orthodoxy." A key feature of the settlement of the iconoclastic controversies was the theological definition of the nature of the icon itself, something deeply remembered today. To avoid the danger of idolatry, icons partake of a series of theological-informed departures from literal reality which show Christ and the saints in their glory, completely transfigured. Rather than show saints in the fallen human condition, icons represent saints in their heavenly condition, showing every trace of the Fall removed and every human trait elevated and consumed by divine life. Their gestures are perfected, their garments restored to supreme harmony, and hair and beards given a stylized perfection. A saint's name is always inscribed on an icon, as the name not only identifies the subject of the icon but establishes the saint's presence.

Most importantly, their faces reveal participation in God's own divine mind, showing a perfected intellect and deep thoughtfulness.

The passions are present but utterly glorified and consumed by grace. So icons require a certain fasting with the eyes, asking the viewer to calm his own desire for emotional stimulation and enter into the desirable yet foreign depths of humanity perfected by God's grace. For similar reasons, iconic figures are never shown with strong raking light across their features from an outside light source like the sun. Rather, they appear to be lit up from within, echoing the description of heaven in Revelation 21:23: it needs no "sun or moon to shine upon it, for the glory of God is its light, and its lamp is the Lamb." The memory of the iconoclastic controversies remains even in newly made icons, and large departures from the established traditions are therefore rare.

The embrace of Peter and Paul, sometimes called the *Concordia Apostolorum*, or concord of the apostles, forms an often-repeated subject in Greek icons. Both saints were instrumental in establishing the early Church, yet each represented differing understandings that were finally settled in the Council of Jerusalem around AD 50. Traditionally, Peter is said to exemplify the Church of the Law inherited from Judaism, particularly its requirement for circumcision, while Paul represents the Church of grace, believing there was no such necessity.[71] In the end, the council settled the question, and so peace was brought to the Church. The embrace of the two men, then, marks more than mere human affection, but a supernatural celestial unity wrought by God.

The challenge for an iconographer is to render unity and deep affection between men in a way that is both fully evident and yet supernaturally restrained. Peter's age is indicated by his white beard and touch of grey hair, while Paul's brown beard falls in curls, perhaps a reference to his status as a Pharisee. The two men stand cheek-to-cheek, a level of intimacy rarely shown in icons other than the embrace between the child Christ and the Virgin. Their mouths are closed, and their eyes display a characteristic lack of brilliance, even amidst their physical and emotional closeness. In a subtle iconic convention, their necks are slightly swollen, indicating the presence of the breath of the Spirit that fills them and joins them in love. Their hug shows a similarly restrained intimacy, as their union in Christ's love is further indicated by their arms resting upon each other's shoulders. It may seem strange at first that their eyes do not meet the other's gaze, yet this pattern is common in icons. The eyes of a saint are fixed on the face of God, so they neither look out at the viewer nor at each other, even in the tenderest moment of unity. So in an utterly transfigured way, Akotantos displays masculine love without the least hint of inappropriateness, displaying for human eyes the unity of two heavenly saints who share an earthly liturgical feast.

Celebrating the Solemnity of Saints Peter and Paul

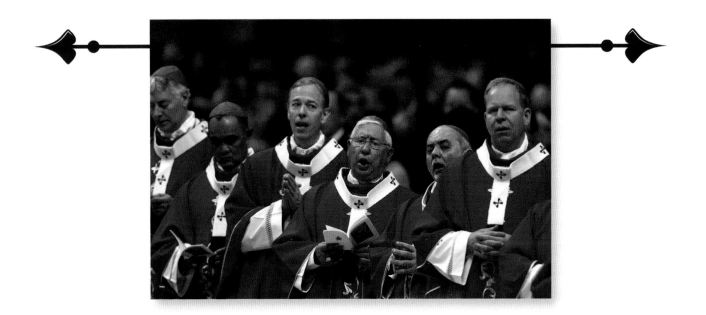

The two "princes of the apostles" are commemorated together on this solemnity, which dates from the earliest centuries of the Church. While they were martyred on different days, it is a longstanding tradition to celebrate these two saints together, echoing the words of St. Paul for the union of Christians. These two saints are the patron saints of Rome, and so this day is kept as a public holiday in Rome, as well as in several other countries around the world.

The Pallium

Each year on this feast day during the papal Mass in Rome, the pope gives the *pallium* to the new metropolitan archbishops from the past year. The pallium is a woolen vestment in the shape of a narrow white band with six black crosses and three gold pins. It is worn by archbishops over their chasuble and looks like a circular scarf with a Y shape. The bottom part of the Y shape is solid black, to symbolize the hoof of the lamb. In his homily on June 29, 2021, Pope Francis explained, "This sign of unity with Peter recalls the mission of the shepherd who gives his life for the flock. It is in giving his life that the shepherd, himself set free, becomes a means of bringing freedom to his brothers and sisters."[72]

The pallium uses a special wool, which has a very interesting story dating back over 500 years. Each year on the feast of St. Agnes, two lambs are brought to the pope for blessing. The lambs are first raised by Trappist monks, and after the blessing they are cared for by the Benedictine nuns at St. Cecilia in Trastevere. After Easter, the lambs are sheared. Their wool is then dried, combed, and spun into yarn for special looms. These textiles are used to make the pallia given to the new bishops by the pope in that same year.

Indulgences for the Feast

A great tradition on this solemnity is for Catholics to visit the cathedral of their diocese or a basilica. There are more than 1,500 basilicas throughout the world, and all celebrate this feast day with a special solemnity. In every basilica, there is an unusual yellow- and red-striped umbrella near the right side of the main altar, known as an *umbraculum*, *ombrellino*, or *conopaeum* (meaning "big umbrella" or canopy), which is presented by the pope when a church is elevated to the status of a basilica. The *umbraculum* remains closed except when the pope himself visits. Traditionally, the *umbraculum* was used for shade for the pope during outdoor processions, so it indicates a special bond of communion with him. A basilica also has a special set of bells mounted on a pole, known as a *tintinnabulum*, which would be carried in procession for Mass with the pope. The *umbraculum*, *tintinnabulum*, and the display of papal insignia of the crossed keys are the three symbols of a church's rank as a minor basilica and are a sign of the unity of the Church.

A plenary indulgence can be gained by those who visit a cathedral or basilica on this solemnity, by faithfully reciting the Our Father and the Creed and then fulfilling the usual conditions: (1) have a detachment from sin, (2) pray for the intentions of the pope, (3) celebrate the sacrament of Reconciliation (confession), and (4) receive the Eucharist. It is appropriate to go to confession and receive the Eucharist on the day the indulgence is sought, but these may be received several days before or after the visit.

Home Altars—A Mirror of the Church

Keeping blessed articles and other devotional items at a family altar or other special location within the home helps remind us of their plentiful uses throughout the year. Some families feel daunted by the idea of a home altar, picturing an elaborate setup, but this can be as simple as a small table, shelf, or wall niche with a crucifix, candles, a family Bible, and special devotional objects, such as statues of patron saints or other holy images. While we know that the Church building is the House of God and place of worship, the home is also a place of prayer, a place of gathering for Christian families. Our domestic Church is a mirror of the universal Church, and the first school of faith.

One of the devotional practices on this solemnity is to make a profession of faith using a blessed object, such as a rosary or religious medal. There is a plenary indulgence associated with this practice if the blessed article has been blessed by a pope or a bishop, and a partial indulgence if it was blessed by a priest.[73] You can recite the Apostles' Creed or the Nicene Creed with the blessed object.

Prayer to Saints Peter and Paul

There is a brief prayer associated with these two great apostles that can be used at any time throughout the year, which can also receive a partial indulgence:

> Holy Apostles Peter and Paul, intercede for us. Guard your people, who rely on the patronage of your apostles Peter and Paul, O Lord, and keep them under your continual protection. Through Christ our Lord. Amen.[74]

The Assumption of the Blessed Virgin Mary

August 15

A great sign appeared in heaven:
a woman clothed with the sun, and the moon beneath her feet,
and on her head a crown of twelve stars.

–Entrance antiphon, Mass during the Day

Like Jesus, Mary's Son—who is the Word in the *beginning*, the Second Adam at the *center* of salvation history, and the Bridegroom whose wedding banquet at the *end* lasts forever—Mary appears to us at the beginning, middle, and end of Sacred Scripture. A type of "second Eve" announced after the Fall, she gives birth to the Savior in time, and at the end of her life is assumed by God to her glorious reward in heaven. Today's Solemnity of the Assumption celebrates her heavenly destiny—and invites us to renew our own desire to achieve this same goal.

Our story begins in the dust of the earth: "The Lord God formed man of dust from the ground, and breathed into his nostrils the breath of life; and man became a living soul" (Genesis 2:7). At the beginning of each Lenten season, as dust is applied to our foreheads on Ash Wednesday, we hear, "Remember that you are dust, and to dust you shall return" (see Genesis 3:19). But Mary's assumption does not leave us in the dust! Rather, she gives us a hope for greater things. As Pope Pius XII addressed Mary in his declaration of the dogma of the Assumption, "It is written, that you appear in beauty, and your virginal body is altogether holy, altogether chaste, altogether the dwelling-place of God; from which it follows that it is not in its nature to decay into *dust*, but that it is transformed, being human, into a glorious and incorruptible life, the same body, living and glorious, unharmed, sharing in perfect life."[75]

Still, the heights Mary assumed remain rooted in the earth, even if she never returns to it. Mary embodies one of the many paradoxes of our faith—namely, that greatness is achieved only through humility. Jesus is the supreme example of such exaltation-via-lowliness. As Paul's letter to the Philippians tells us, "Though he was in the form of God, [he] did not count equality with God a thing to be grasped, but emptied himself, taking the form of a servant, being born in the likeness of men. And being found in human form he humbled himself and became obedient unto death, even death on a cross. Therefore, God has highly exalted him and bestowed on him the name which is above every name" (Philippians 2:6–9). You may recall that the words "humility" and "human" share a common root—*humus*, or earth, dirt. Only by realizing who we are and what God made us to be on earth will we reach our supernatural life in heaven.

Mary's humility, like her Son's, launches her into the heavens at her Assumption. The readings and prayers of the day's liturgies make this point clear. The Church's Opening Prayer for the Vigil Mass combines both humility and glory in the praise of the Mother of God: "O God, who, looking on the *lowliness* of the Blessed Virgin

Mary, *raised* her to this grace." But the pinnacle of Mary's lowliness resounds in the Magnificat ("My soul magnifies") upon her visit to Elizabeth, read at the gospel during Mass during the day.

Before looking briefly at this text (which has been prayed at Evening Prayer around the world for centuries), we should note that another of her lowly attributes also leads to her greatness and ultimate Assumption: her obedience. To *obey* means "to hear," and in Mary's case, this meant to hear the message of God. Today, as in all times throughout history, obedience is not deemed so much a virtue as it is a vice for the weak-willed and slavish. But Mary's greatness grows out of her obedience. Obey the Word, conceive the Word. "You are blessed," says St. Ambrose on the doorstep of Christmas, "because you have heard and believed. A soul that believes both conceives and brings forth the Word of God and acknowledges his works."[76] Rather than listening to herself and her own will, Mary obediently believes an authority greater than herself. And for this credulity, her reward is magnificent.

It was obedience, too, which led Mary to visit her cousin Elizabeth. When Mary learned of her cousin's miraculous pregnancy, she immediately left to visit her. After Elizabeth greets her with the words, "Blessed is she who believed that there would be a fulfillment of what was spoken to her from the Lord" (Luke 1:45), Mary begins her magnificent hymn of praise to the Father: "My soul magnifies the Lord, and my spirit rejoices in God my Savior, for he has regarded the *low estate* of his handmaiden. For behold, henceforth all generations will call me blessed…. [H]e has put down the mighty from their thrones, and exalted those of *low degree*" (Luke 1:46–48, 52). Is it because Mary considered herself the lowliest of God's subjects that he would eventually raise her to the very greatness of the Lord?

Pope Pius XII thought so. In 1950, after consultation with all of the bishops of the world, he declared the Assumption of the lowly Blessed Virgin Mary into heaven a dogma of the Church: "By the authority of our Lord Jesus Christ, of the Blessed Apostles Peter and Paul, and by our own authority, we pronounce, declare, and define it to be a divinely revealed dogma: that the Immaculate Mother of God, the ever Virgin Mary, having completed the course of her earthly life, was assumed body and soul into heavenly glory."[77] Along with Mary's assumption, the Church's Liturgy exhorts us to imitate her glory: "Today the Virgin Mother of God was assumed into heaven as the beginning and image of your Church's coming to perfection and a sign of sure hope and comfort to your pilgrim people."[78] Thus, may we—like Christ, like Mary—by our lowliness be brought, body and soul, to the glories of heaven.

The Assumption of the Virgin by Ambrogio da Fossano (known as Bergognone) (c. 1522) oil and gold on wood, Metropolitan Museum of Art, New York

In *Lumen Gentium*, the document of the Second Vatican Council on the nature of the Church, the Assumption of the Virgin is portrayed as a kind of bookend with her Immaculate Conception. Because she was "free from all guilt of original sin," she was "taken up body and soul into heavenly glory, and exalted by the Lord as Queen of the universe."[79] But, as in all Marian doctrines, the Virgin participates in a singular way in the redemption wrought by Christ, whose resurrected body was called the "first fruits of those who have fallen asleep" (1 Corinthians 15:20). Those who follow him will also share, in time, in a body which will not decay, and therefore live forever in glory. The first application of Christ's victory over death—of both spirit and body—was given to the Virgin, initially in her conception, and later at the end of her earthly life, when her uncorrupted body was taken to heaven.

Painter Ambrogio da Fassano, known by his nickname Bergognone, worked largely in and around the northern Italian city of Milan, with the 1522 *Assumption* being the last work of his life. Though his lifespan falls squarely within the Italian Renaissance, his work preserves some medieval characteristics, such as a hierarchical arrangement packed with carefully placed figures, gemlike colors, and careful attention to secondary details. He follows a long line of artists who portrayed the Assumption, since the feast is known to have existed in the Eastern Church—where it is called the Dormition of Mary—as early as the 6th century. The Church has never made a firm determination on whether the Virgin died peacefully or "fell asleep," as the term dormition implies, but in either case, she was freed from the need to suffer bodily decay in order to find the full glory of heaven.

At the bottom of the painting, the apostles form a nearly rectangular mass, appearing only from the waist up and wearing clothing of gold, emerald green, and ruby red. While they raise their eyes in amazement at the dramatic scene before them, they retain the sadness coming from seeing the Mother of God taken from their midst. Located between the apostles and the heavenly beings above lies the hilly landscape outside of Jerusalem, with its city walls and gates, as well as a prominent stony mountain, traditionally a place of encounter between God and man. Exactly where the earthly sky ends and the heavens begin remains unclear, showing a seamless intersection between heaven and earth which characterizes the Virgin herself.

Carried by angels in golden robes, she stands on a cloud, hands folded in prayerful humility, with long hair falling upon her shoulders. This arrangement explicitly recalls the traditional iconography of the Immaculate Conception, which preceded and assured the Assumption. But now, rather than descending as in the Immaculate Conception, she is being raised up to the waiting embrace of

Christ. Mary commands the painting like a great vertical column, though the angels around her form the traditional almond shape known as a mandorla, a gate-like edge marking the intersection of heaven and earth. Her face is slightly downcast, indicating her humility, yet her eyes are fixed on Christ. In a convention easy to overlook, the Virgin's body is elongated, with her waist and legs nearly twice the length of her upper body. This idealization indicates the perfection of her earthly body, just as Christ's nearly triangular shape denotes his divinity as the second person of the Trinity. The stars upon the Virgin's sapphire-blue garment are actual three-dimensional metal appliques, symbolizing her exalted title as Queen of Heaven. In a virtuosic move, Bergognone painted text appearing embroidered into the golden border of her mantle, including words from the *Pater Noster* and *Ave Maria*.

Nearly fifty angels appear in the painting, dressed differently and doing different things. One of the accounts of the Assumption in the thirteenth-century *Golden Legend* mentions that when Christ came to bring his mother to heaven, he came with "melody and song" as well as the "orders of the angels." Music has traditionally been thought to be the heavenly version of sound, which, with word, meter, harmony, and rhythm, revealed to the ear the sound of the restored earth and the perfection of heaven. The angels closest to Christ appear less corporeal and somewhat hazy, with only faces and blue wings highlighted in gold. As the angels move down the hierarchy, they become more bodily. Five angels on each side of Christ's hands—dressed in white, green, and red, the colors representing faith, hope, and charity—sing from an unrolled scroll of written music with realistic notation. Below them, another group of angels plays instrumental music on lutes and harps, which, though it adds its harmony to heaven, does not include the human voice, and so is lower in the hierarchy of song. Below them, angels blow trumpets to announce the Assumption, each instrument bedecked with a white flag with the red Cross of Saint Ambrose, the symbol of the city of Milan. But the largest angels are those dressed in white who place the crown of queenship on the Virgin, as they, too, seem to dwell within the embrace of Christ.

Although Bergognone's painting highlights the singular honors given to the Mother of God, the promise of the Assumption applies to all who accept God's offer of salvation. She is glorified above all other creatures, yet the Virgin does not become a goddess. In the *Assumption* she retains her humility, her humanity, and even her clothes. But in Christ's victory, they all become transfigured. The glorification of the body was made real first by the Resurrection of Christ, the new Adam, and second in his mother, the New Eve. The promise for all Christians, then, is that this same victory will be applied in time to all of creation. So Bergognone's *Assumption* is therefore a reminder that God's promises will be fulfilled and becomes a beacon of hope for all.

Celebrating the Assumption of the Blessed Virgin Mary

This solemnity has been known by several names throughout the history of the Church: the Assumption of the Blessed Virgin Mary, the Dormition of the Virgin, and the Virgin's Repose. It was originally celebrated on January 18 but was moved to its present date in the sixth century. Devotion to Mary as the *Theotokos* is an ancient tradition in the Church, and there is some evidence of a feast day on August 15 dedicated to Mary under the title of "God-bearer."[80] Today, the feast of Mary, Mother of God on January 1 focuses on this aspect of Marian devotion, while August 15 celebrated her bodily assumption into heaven.

The Drama of This Feast

One of the great festivals held around the world on this day is celebrated in Spain. Mary is said to have given a special blessing to the town of Elche, near Alicante—she delivered "her miraculous image over the sea in a chest inscribed: 'Soy para Elche.'"[81] Subsequently, her image was enshrined in the cathedral of the diocese. The story of this image inspired the operetta *The Mystery of Elche*, and the feast of the Assumption was marked by an annual performance of this operetta in the cathedral. In the re-enactment, the figure of Mary processes into the cathedral surrounded by angels, and she is then handed a golden palm by an angel from heaven, symbolizing her passing from this life. Mary's deathbed is surrounded by the apostles, and then she disappears, replaced by that miraculous image. The following day, surrounded by candles, the image is taken in procession. The final dramatic element has "the Virgin herself being taken up into heaven, being slowly drawn up amid figures of saints and angels, and received her crown from God the Father to the sound of bells and other musical instruments: the crowd, now wild with excitement, praying, weeping, and applauding enthusiastically."[82]

A Marian Lent

In the Eastern tradition, the feast of the Dormition is preceded by a period of fasting for fifteen days. This tradition can also be observed in the West, a "Little Lent of Mary," as a reminder to be open to receiving the good gifts from God. Every time we fast, we prepare our bodies and souls to receive what God has prepared for us. Just as Mary was receptive to hearing the word of God, responding to him and receiving him, we too can prepare our hearts and minds to truly hear God's word.

Blessing of Herbs, First Fruits, and Harvest

Traditionally on this solemnity, families bring fresh herbs to the church to be blessed. In some places within the Greek tradition, the offering would include new wheat as a symbol of first fruits. The blessing of herbs was found in previous versions of the *Roman Ritual* for this feast day. It continues to be a part of the Church's life and is mentioned in the *Directory on Popular Piety and the Liturgy*, which explains, "one must turn to God, through whose word 'the earth produced vegetation: plants bearing seeds in their several kinds, and trees bearing fruit with their seed inside in their several kinds' (Genesis 1:12)." Many of the common symbols for Our Lady include the lily, the vine, and other images taken from Sacred Scripture, due to the sweetness of her virtue and her motherhood of the Christ child. She is, after all, the "Root of Jesse," who will bear Jesus as the "blessed fruit of her womb." The prayer in the *Roman Ritual* helps us to understand this beautiful connection between the fruits of the earth and the motherhood of Mary:

> Let us pray.
> God, who on this day raised up to highest heaven the rod of Jesse,
> the Mother of your Son, our Lord Jesus Christ,
> that by her prayers and patronage you might communicate to our mortal nature
> the fruit of her womb, your very Son;
> we humbly implore you to help us use these fruits of the soil
> for our temporal and everlasting welfare,
> aided by the power of your Son
> and the prayers of his glorious Mother;
> through Christ our Lord. Amen.

If you would like to pray in your own garden, *Catholic Household Blessings and Prayers* gives the following description: "On August 15 … the produce of fields, gardens, and orchards may be blessed. Those who take part should assemble in an appropriate place around the grains, fruits, and vegetables to be blessed." One option for a prayer that you may use at home is taken from the "Occasion of Thanksgiving for the Harvest." If your parish offers a blessing of flowers and herbs, bring your family to the blessing with some special plants. Bringing these gifts to the Church represents our gratitude to God for the gifts that he has given to us in the fruits of the earth and in all his benefits. It serves as a reminder that we should continually praise him for these gifts, after the pattern of Abel.

The Gifts of Creation

A popular tradition in many Catholic households is to plant a "Mary garden." In many places, this would be done in the month of May, as a particular month set aside in prayer to Mary. Consider preparing a garden dedicated to Mary and visit it on this solemnity, as well as on other Marian feasts and special occasions throughout the year. Many Mary gardens include flowers and herbs of biblical significance, such as the rose, the lily, and lavender. Make a list of things you are grateful for as a family, in gratitude for the gifts of the earth, such as flowers, herbs, fruits, and vegetables, reminding us of God's care for all his creation. Flowing from the celebration of Mass, pray a family rosary concluding with the singing of the *Salve Regina* or the popular hymn *Hail, Holy Queen*.

All Saints

November 1

I looked, and behold, a great multitude which no man could number, from every nation, from all tribes and peoples and tongues.

–Revelation 7:9

God calls every person to be a saint. Sanctity—which means thinking, loving, and living like Jesus—is not an optional goal meant only for a select few. The Solemnity of All Saints, celebrated on November 1, reminds us of our glorious calling in Christ.

The Church recalls for us on this day that the saints are not limited to those now bearing the title "saint" by us on earth. To be sure, St. Peter, St. Thérèse of Lisieux, and St. Francis of Assisi are truly, definitely, *saints*, as their official canonization by the Church attests. But so too are those among the "great multitude which no man could number, from every nation, from all tribes and peoples and tongues" (Revelation 7:9; first reading from Mass). That is, all in heaven are saints, regardless of whether they are officially recognized as such by the Church. The Preface of the Mass of the day suggests the same: "Today by your gift we celebrate the festival of your city, the heavenly Jerusalem, our mother, where the great array of our brothers and sisters already gives you eternal praise." The price of heavenly citizenship is sanctity.

This insight—that only saints live in heaven—might give us pause. Anyone reading this book is hopefully planning on reaching heaven. If we follow the Church's teaching, attend Mass each Sunday, pray regularly, and practice charity, our chances are good for heavenly admittance. But how many of us hopeful for heaven are also aiming to become saints? If we think that heaven is possible without being a saint—that is, without being holy—then we are not thinking with the mind of the Church.

A key lesson of the Solemnity of All Saints, then, teaches us to desire sanctity above all else while we work toward our heavenly home. We should think of the Solemnity of All Saints as *our own* future feast day. St. Bernard of Clairvaux (1090–1153) speaks in the Office of Readings for the Solemnity of how its observance inflames him with a "tremendous yearning" to be with the saints and "share in the citizenship of heaven." We might feel the same—at least for a time. "But our dispositions change," he admits. "The Church of all the first followers of Christ awaits us, but we do nothing about it. The saints want us to be with them, and we are indifferent. The souls of the just await us, and we ignore them." So, if simply seeking sanctity from time to time is insufficient, what should we do? If we wish to be with the saints, we must know what they did to become saints, and then ask ourselves how to follow their example.

The common denominator among the saints is their likeness to Christ. Indeed, in the beginning, God created us in his image and likeness (see Genesis 1:26). Subsequent sin disfigured us, and personal sin continues to do so. Christ comes not only as a model for us but also sends his Spirit and his grace to work a wonderful transformation that reshapes us in his image. Every saint is a unique personality, but every saint has also become a living, breathing reflection of Jesus. St. John tells us in the second reading from Mass that "we shall be like him, for we shall see him as he is" (1 John 3:2). By keeping Christ before our eyes, and aided by his grace, "we shall be like him" as saints.

But it is also important to understand why the Church recognizes a hierarchy among the saints. The greatest saints are the martyrs, for they are like Christ not only in their lives but also in their deaths. After the first Christian centuries, the Church saw a pause in the Roman persecution of her members. As a result, the faithful less frequently saw martyrdom as a way to conform themselves to Christ in both life and death, and they turned to other means of sanctity, especially an asceticism which highlighted death to self and to the world. Those who lived such a life and died a natural death were likewise venerated as saints. St. Anthony of the Desert (251–356) and St. Martin of Tours (316–397) are among the most renowned among these kinds of saints.

The first reading from the book of Revelation today emphasizes the saints' imitation of Christ not only in life but in death. Those who surround the throne of God, it says, "are they who have come out of the great tribulation; they have washed their robes and made them white in the blood of the Lamb" (Revelation 7:14). In the early centuries in Rome, in fact, the celebration of the collective body of saints and martyrs was observed in the springtime of the year, closer to the Paschal Mystery of Jesus, and many Eastern Churches continue to commemorate the martyrs around the time that the Church celebrates Christ's death and resurrection.

While God may not be calling each of us to be martyrs, all Catholics are washed in the blood of the Lamb—first in Baptism, then in the Eucharist. As we should expect, there is an intimate connection between the death and resurrection of Jesus, the Eucharist, and sanctity. Traditionally, for example, each church altar contained the relic of a martyr (although relics of saints who were not martyred are now permissible). It is the martyrs, however, who most clearly connect sanctity with the Eucharist. For like the martyrs, the Eucharistic bread and wine manifest the dying and rising of Christ before our eyes. Ultimately, the best way to participate in the life and death of Christ, achieve sanctity, and appreciate those we remember on All Saints is to become martyrs; the second-best way is to receive the Eucharist worthily.

"Let us all rejoice in the Lord," the Mass's entrance antiphon announces, "as we celebrate the feast day in honor of all the Saints, at whose festival the Angels rejoice and praise the Son of God." Truly, the solemnity of All Saints is a joyful day: a day to rejoice in the salvation won by Christ; a day to rejoice in those who have lived holy lives; a day to rejoice in our own call to sanctity.

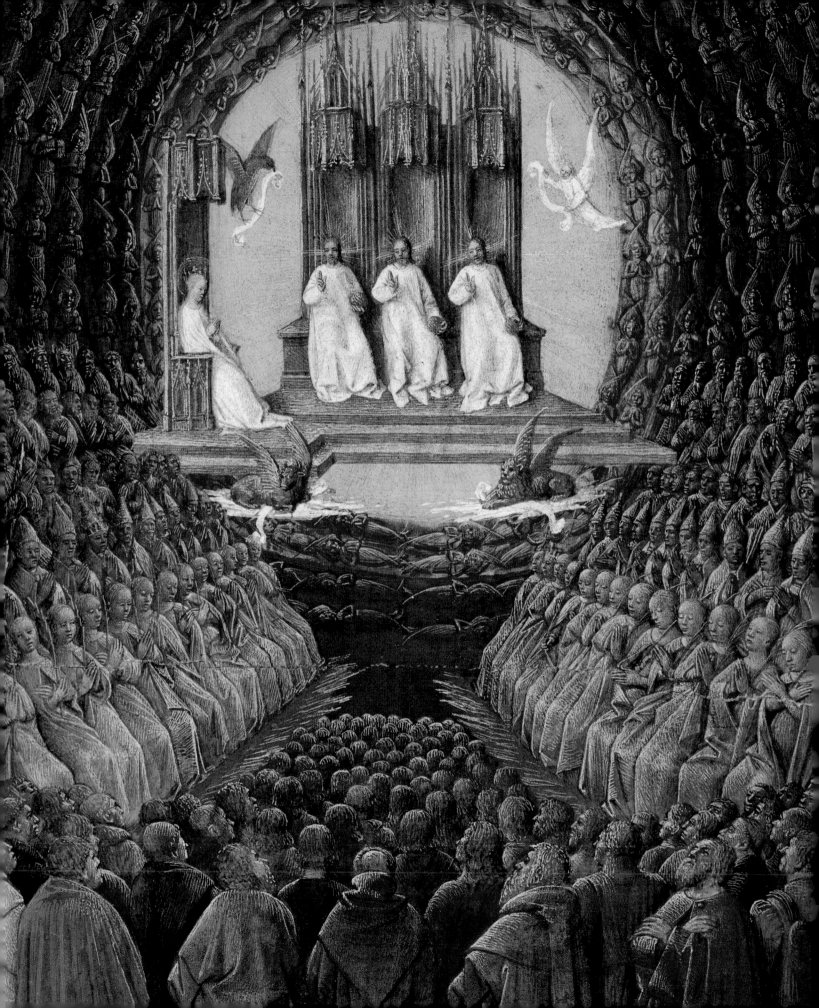

The Trinity in Its Glory from the Hours of Étienne Chevalier by Jean Fouquet
(c. 1452) Musée Condé, Chantilly, France

When St. John experienced his vision of heaven in the book of Revelation, he saw the throne of God surrounded by multitudes that no one could count, from every tribe and nation of the world (see Revelation 7:9). Together with angels and four mysterious winged creatures, he saw saints forming a great choir singing God's praises. He had already seen the colorful, jewel-like throne of God surrounded by white-robed elders (Revelation 4), and in a third vision, he saw heaven as a great city of gem-covered walls which needed no sun because it was lit by the glory of Christ. Long before the Church had established a feast of all saints, John had seen them in one sweeping vision, and artists and theologians have used his mystical account as a model ever since.

In the mid-fifteenth century, painter Jean Fouquet captured the magnificence of God and his saints in an image just under eight inches tall. Relatively little is known about Fouquet's life, but his tremendous talent had given him the opportunity to create a portrait of Pope Eugene IV and become court painter of King Louis XI. Around 1452, he was hired by the French royal treasurer, Étienne Chevalier, to provide illuminations for a personal book of hours, a book containing prayers said at different times of day. Though the book was split up and its pages were separated in the eighteenth century, forty-seven of Fouquet's images survive, illustrating feasts from the Church year and different events of sacred history. The Trinity in Its Glory is believed by scholars to have come toward the end of the book, providing something of a summary of the year's feasts, showing all saints are assembled before the throne of God.

Fouquet was admired for the amazingly precise detail in his works, and this vision of heaven was no exception. A careful observer would be hard-pressed to count the angels and saints, whose individual faces are distinguishable despite being a mere quarter of an inch high. At the center, golden light emanates from the persons of the Trinity on a triple throne, recalling the Gothic canopies of medieval cathedrals, while the Blessed Virgin sits on her own throne to the left, signifying her privileged position as the Queen of All Saints. It may appear at first that three Christs occupy the throne rather than the expected white-bearded Father and the dove of the Holy Spirit. This convention, more common in Eastern icons, uses Christ as the image of the Father since Christ said to St. Philip, "He who has seen me has seen the Father" (John 14:9). In this way, the image stays deeply biblical while emphasizing God's unfathomable majesty.

At the corners of the throne appear the four winged creatures, each with a different form: an ox, a lion, an eagle, and the face of a man. From the earliest centuries of Christianity, these strange creatures were understood as symbolic images of the four evangelists. The eagle recalls the soaring theology of the Gospel of John, which opens with the proclamation of Christ's divinity. The ox signifies Luke's Gospel, which speaks of Christ in relation to the Jerusalem Temple and its animal sacrifices. Matthew's Gospel traces Christ's human genealogy and so is represented by a human face, while the lion indicates the beginning of the Gospel of Mark, where John the Baptist calls out in the wilderness like a roaring lion. The leadership role of these principal saints is indicated as well, since whenever the winged creatures sing "holy, holy, holy" before God, the other heavenly beings fall down and do the same (Revelation 4:6–11).

The light of the Trinity illuminates and transfigures all of heaven and its saints, and a close inspection reveals that the red circle around the throne is constituted by two rows of winged angels with their hands folded in prayer, appearing with a gem-like radiance and fiery light. Beyond them appear seven circles of sapphire-colored angels, completing the famed nine choirs who praise and serve God. Closer to the viewer sit the many white-robed multitudes whose garments appear gold in the glorious light of God. The virgin martyrs appear in the front rows, holding palm branches as the sign of their sacrifice. Each tiny martyr shows a slightly different pose and expression, marking their individuality even amidst the great unity of saints. In the rows behind, saints of different categories appear as well, some wearing bishops' miters, others the crowns of kings. Some show papal tiaras, and others the bare heads of the laity. At the left the crowned figure of King David can be seen sitting next to Moses with the biblical rays of light emerging from his head. At the bottom appear saints more contemporary to 1450, recognizable by the habits of their religious orders, such as the Cistercian dressed in white at the lower left. At the lower right, contemporary, well-dressed laymen—people who serve Christ in the world—appear as well.

Interestingly, this masterful image almost reads like a building, where the angels and saints appear to form the stones and statues of a great cathedral doorway, with the newer saints walking to the throne of God amidst a joyful welcome. This is no coincidence, since Scripture speaks of Christians as living stones in God's building (1 Corinthians 3:9–13). Just as a church building is composed of many parts hierarchically assembled, so the saints form a great image of Christ's body (John 2:21), enlivened by divine life and brought to intimate union with God the Father. So a saint arranged in the great choir of heaven lives in ecstatic delight, prays for those still on earth, and praises God with an intensity born of the deepest possible gratitude for being rescued from death and brought into the radiant life of the Trinity. And Fouquet's mastery of art makes this unfathomable reality visible to the human eye, allowing earthly Christians to get a foretaste of their own future, inspiring them to say yes to God's generous offer of eternal bliss.

Celebrating the Solemnity of All Saints

Popular customs surrounding this solemnity are wrapped up in the larger celebration of three days, "All Saints-tide," from the eve of All Saints to All Souls Day. Devotional practices in the domestic church and popular piety flow from the combination of these liturgical days as they point to the same ultimate goal—eternal life.

The Remembrance of the Dead

In various cultures around the world, it is a custom to visit the cemetery on All Saints as well as All Souls. The Mexican observance of *Día de los Muertos* is marked by visiting graves of deceased relatives and decorating with flowers, crosses, and garlands. Louisiana folklore recounts similar customs: grave markers were whitewashed and cleaned on *Toussaint*, crowned with a wreath of waxed paper flowers. Loved ones lit candles at the graveside in the late afternoon as it gets close to dark in vigil for their deceased relatives and friends.

In many countries, All Saints is also a public holiday, including in some parts of Germany. In Mainz, *Allerheiligen* and *Allerseelen* are commemorated with a special type of candle unique to the area. The *Newweling* is referenced as early as 1347 and continues to be crafted today. It is made with candle wicks dipped in wax, usually in two colors, and the two wicks are wrapped around a cone shape. These short candles, about three to six inches tall, are placed on gravestones in remembrance of the deceased.

Around the world, visits to the cemetery help us to remember and pray for our deceased loved ones. This custom also helps the living to contemplate saintly models, both known and unknown, and put our own mortality into perspective. A visit to the cemetery can be simple, and a good practice for entire families. There is a solemn order for visiting the cemetery in the *Book of Blessings*. Many parishes in the US and Canada preserve this practice each year or celebrate Mass at the cemetery on All Souls. *Catholic Household Blessings and Prayers* contains an order of prayer for individual use when visiting a grave. When you make a visit to the cemetery on either day, perhaps bringing flowers to the grave of loved ones, or lighting a candle, these prayers can be used along with a litany of the saints.

Litany of the Saints

It is a most fitting practice to sing the litany of saints together on this day. A litany is an ancient style of prayer with a series of invocations and a repeated response. This can be sung or said at the Church, at night prayer, or even in the popular practice of a procession of saints on this feast day, where children dress up as their patron saint, or favorite saint. A domestic litany of the saints can include saints that are special to the family, whether patrons or namesakes that are saints recognized by the Church. In coming to know the saints and learning their stories, we see that it is possible, through Christ, for us to come to the same heavenly glory. The saints are both historical witnesses and disciples of Christ, but are now citizens of the heavenly Jerusalem. Becoming familiar with this practice at home also serves as a reminder of the key moments in the life of the Christian: the litany of saints is used at the Easter Vigil, at Baptisms, ordinations, and religious professions, as well as in other important liturgical celebrations. The traditional litany of the saints has a particular order: first we invoke the intercession of Mary, then the angels and archangels, patriarchs and prophets (including St. Joseph), apostles and martyrs, bishops and doctors of the church, pastors and religious, holy men and women, pray for us!

A Hymn of Praise: For All the Saints

Perhaps at Mass on this Holy Day, you have sung the familiar hymn "For All the Saints." This hymn is included in nearly every hymnal published in the English language in the past century. It is easy to look up the sheet music or a recording, as it is widely available—perhaps you can sing it together as a family or listen to a recording of it at home on this solemnity. Originally eleven verses, five verses are commonly used in today's hymnals. Penned in 1864 by William H. How, the text bore the original title "Saints' Day Hymn: A Cloud of Witnesses," with a reference to the first verse of chapter twelve of the letter to the Hebrews. "Therefore, since we are surrounded by so great a cloud of witnesses, let us rid ourselves of every burden and sin that clings to us and persevere in running the race that lies before us while keeping our eyes fixed on Jesus, the leader and perfecter of faith" (Hebrews 12:1–2). The emphasis of this hymn reminds us of the crown of glory won by the apostles and martyrs, of that joyful communion of saints, and of the importance of perseverance in the Christian life. The last stanzas help us to focus on that vision of heavenly worship, of that great multitude of the saints and countless angels gathered around the throne, singing the eternal hymn of praise (see Revelation 7:9).

> For all the saints who from their labors rest,
> who thee by faith before the world confessed,
> thy name, O Jesus, be forever blest.
> Alleluia, alleluia!
>
> Thou wast their rock, their fortress, and their might;
> thou, Lord, their captain in the well fought fight;
> thou in the darkness drear their one true light.
> Alleluia, alleluia!
>
> O blest communion, fellowship divine!
> We feebly struggle, they in glory shine;
> yet all are one in thee, for all are thine.
> Alleluia, alleluia!
>
> And when the strife is fierce, the warfare long,
> steals on the ear the distant triumph song,
> and hearts are brave again, and arms are strong.
> Alleluia, alleluia!
>
> From earth's wide bounds,
>   from ocean's farthest coast,
> through gates of pearl
>   streams in the countless host,
> singing to Father, Son, and Holy Ghost:
> Alleluia, alleluia!

Our Lord Jesus Christ, King of the Universe
(Christ the King)

Last Sunday in Ordinary Time

We shall enter the kingdom of heaven,
because while we lived on earth we acknowledged heaven's King.

–St. Hippolytus of Rome, Office of Readings on December 30

The final solemnity of the Church's liturgical year celebrates Our Lord Jesus Christ, King of the Universe, commonly called simply Christ the King. In a certain sense, each of the year's solemn celebrations, like all times and all events, have been oriented toward this observance. Christ is the King of heaven, of earth, and of every heart (if we allow it).

Three previous solemnities shed light on Christ the King. First, the solemnity of the Epiphany can be considered the original observance of Christ's kingship. On this day, we heard how the battle of kings—between King Herod, the kingdoms of the earth, and the newborn infant king—is won by Christ: "Behold, the Lord, the Mighty One, has come; and kingship is in his grasp, and power and dominion."[83] Epiphany, then, is our first introduction to our Lord's reign.

The second solemnity, located near the mid-point of the liturgical year, is the Sacred Heart of Jesus. In 1925, in his encyclical establishing the feast of Christ the King, Pope Pius XI asks that "the dedication of mankind to the Sacred Heart of Jesus … be made annually on that day."[84] God reigns as King of Love, his heart loving our hearts, and our hearts coming to beat in unison with his. Our celebration of his rule at year's end places all that we have—our prayers, works, joys, and sufferings, as we pray in the Morning Offering in honor of the Sacred Heart—under his rule, especially our love.

Near the end of the liturgical year, the Solemnity of All Saints is the third celebration that helps us understand and pray the Solemnity of Christ the King. In Pius XI's above-mentioned encyclical introducing this solemnity, he placed it "on the last Sunday of the month of October—the Sunday, that is, which immediately precedes the Feast of All Saints." But wherever its location on the liturgical calendar—the end of October or, as at present, the final Sunday of the liturgical year—its connection to the saints should call to our minds how Christ rules in the saintly heart. In today's Office of Readings, the Church Father Origen (c. 185–253) speaks of the saint's heart as a "kind of spiritual paradise where God may walk and be [its] sole ruler with his Christ."

As these previous solemnities indicate, the Kingdom of God is one of lowliness and humility (Epiphany), love (Sacred Heart), and holiness (All Saints). The preface text for the Mass of the day goes on to call this "eternal and universal kingdom" a "kingdom of truth and life, a kingdom of holiness and grace, a kingdom of justice, love and peace." And if you live in such a kingdom, you are, like its ruler, a priest. Jesus' priesthood is another key aspect of this day, for it is a central feature of Christ's kingship—and ours.

Some of history's kings are peaceful, some are warriors. Some kings are wise, and some are compassionate. Many kings are wealthy, and most are powerful. Each of these descriptors can be said of our King. But more fundamental than any of these kingly attributes is Jesus' priesthood—he is a king who is also a priest. The preface for the Mass ties Jesus' kingship to his priesthood: "For you anointed your Only Begotten Son, our Lord Jesus Christ, with the oil of gladness as eternal Priest and King of all creation." The entrance antiphon for the Mass attributes "power and divinity, and wisdom and strength and honor" to Christ the King as he rules as "the Lamb who was slain." Even Christ's subjects, since they have been conformed to him in Baptism, are also kings and priests, living eternally in his "kingdom, priests to his God and Father" (Revelation 1:6; second reading during Year B). This priestly kingdom is unlike any on earth. It is one where Christ and his followers offer their whole selves to the Father in the Spirit for the world's redemption and the Trinity's glory. "My kingship is not of this world; if my kingship were of this world, my servants would fight, that I might not be handed over to the Jews; but my kingship is not from the world" (John 18:36).

Baptism opens the door to this kingdom, and a life governed by Christ and his teaching must follow. "If we wish God to reign in us," writes Origen in the Office of Readings for the day, "in no way *should sin reign in our mortal body*; rather we should *mortify our members which are upon the earth* and bear fruit in the Spirit." We should, in other words, exercise Christ's kingship within us while on earth so that one day we might reign with him in heaven. In the *Catechism*, we have the description of St. Ambrose (c. 339–397) of the Christian king: "That man is rightly called a king who makes his own body an obedient subject and, by governing himself with suitable rigor, refuses to let his passions breed rebellion in his soul, for he exercises a kind of royal power over himself" (CCC 908). If we can rule ourselves with Christ's aid, the kingdom of God can be a land where we live even now. As Origen writes, "Anyone who is holy obeys the spiritual laws of God, who dwells in him as in a well-ordered city. The Father is present in the perfect soul, and with him Christ reigns."[85]

So as the Church's year comes to a close, we pray that the many graces that have been offered us through the cycle's solemnities have "transferred us to the kingdom of his beloved Son" (Colossians 1:13). The Solemnity of Our Lord Jesus Christ, King of the Universe honors our priestly ruler, welcomes our membership in his kingdom, and grants us our freedom from slavery to sin.

May Jesus reign now and forever!

Christic in Majesty from the *Last Judgment Mosaic*, artist unknown
(thirteenth century) Baptistery, Florence

The idea of Christ's final judgment of humanity has taken on an air of fear over the centuries, often inspired by the heresy of Jansenism and its subsequent piety which hyperemphasized God's demanding standards and man's unworthiness. Yet the Christ of the Florence baptistery, while certainly presented as the powerful King of heaven and earth, is neither angry nor fearsome, even as some souls are led to hell by demons. Though Christ is as tall as a two-and-a-half-story building, his face is kind. Though he clearly has the power over life and death, he is calm and ordered. His power shows the strength of *wrath*, which is not moody anger, but God's desire to set things right and restore the world by defeating the power of death. Therefore, Christ's power is the flip side of his love; without power, his love would be incapable of bringing creation back to the Father. Christ's Last Judgment, then, is good news for the world—at last the application of the restoration wrought by the Paschal Mystery is complete.

The vision of Christ in majesty comes from chapter four of the book of Revelation, where St. John is taken up into ecstasy and gets a view of heaven. He sees "a throne … with one seated on the throne," where Christ appeared like "jasper and carnelian, and round the throne was a rainbow that looked like an emerald" (Revelation 4:2–3). Christ's divinity is on vivid display, since from the throne came "flashes of lightning, and voices and peals of thunder" (Revelation 4:5), both biblical signs of God's presence. A throne is also a marker of authority and kingship, and so through it, Christ is not only honored as redeemer and God but as the one with the authority to separate the sheep from the goats and therefore crush the power of sin and death. John's note that he appears like jasper and carnelian also carries rich symbolic meaning. The high priest in the Old Testament wore a breastplate studded with twelve gems, each representing one of the tribes of Israel. These tribes symbolized the chosen people, who themselves stood in for all of humanity. Interestingly, carnelian was the first stone on the breastplate, representing the tribe of Reuben. Jasper was the last stone, representing the tribe of Benjamin, the youngest and last of the sons of Israel. Christ, then, who describes himself as the alpha and the omega, the beginning and the end, is now shown to have restored all of humanity, from the first tribe to the last.

This gem-like radiance of heavenly things reveals an important thread of symbolism flowing through Scripture. The radiance of gems signified that matter has been brought to its heavenly perfection, much as sooty carbon is transformed into diamond. 1 Peter 2:5 speaks of Christians as "living stones" in the temple of God, his poetic name for people who are shaped and polished by God, then infused with divine life. Later, the walls of heaven are described as having foundations made of gems as well (Revelation 21:19–20), meaning heaven is made of saints, who, like gems, are radiant with the light of Christ. To read that Christ sat on a rainbow also recalls the great sign given to Noah at the end of the Flood, a mark of reconciliation between God and humanity. So stones are people brought to glory, and these people are the reconciled members of Christ's Body; when properly assembled, they form his image. In a delightful symbolic continuity, the artistic medium of mosaic does the same thing. Unlike a painting, a mosaic is made of tiny pieces of colored stone and glass called *tessare*, each approximately the size of a fingernail. Their similarity to gems is obvious, yet they only find their revelatory fulfillment when properly assembled, and the face of Christ literally appears.

This inherited theology is put on display at the Florence baptistery. The gem-patterned circle around Christ is a round mandorla, the traditional marker of the opening between heaven and earth through which, like John, we see God's glory. Yet Christ appears both in heaven *and* earth. His head sits in front of the mandorla, as does his right foot, indicating his action in the realm of creation. Yet the rest of his body rests in heaven, sitting on the emerald rainbow. Christ's pose is therefore dynamic even as it appears restful and carefully arranged, partaking of a traditional iconic convention. The upper part of Christ's body appears exactly parallel to the viewer, while his lower body turns with one foot in front of the other. Here Christ's unquestionably peaceful perfection combines with his dynamic salvific activity. His clothing also partakes of a convention of Eastern icons. Not only are they trimmed in gold—called adding the "fire" of divine perfection to matter—but the red of his full tunic symbolizes his divinity, while the blue garment laid upon it his humanity. So even the garments speak of Christ's reality: the divine Second Person of the Trinity "put on" humanity in the Incarnation, becoming one person with two natures.

In an unusual move, Christ's hands are presented asymmetrically, with his right hand facing up and his left hand facing down. These correspond to small images below the circle, where on the viewer's left, the souls of the saved rise from their tombs and enter heaven. Under Christ's downward-facing left hand, the souls of the damned are led off to eternal separation from God. Not coincidentally, this great image appears in a baptistery, where the Christian dies to self in Baptism and rises again in new life in Christ. The rest of his or her life becomes a series of choices and actions under the watchful eye of the loving God to choose him and attain salvation, becoming a living stone in the glorious temple which is his heavenly body.

Celebrating the Solemnity of Christ the King

As we have seen, Pope Pius XI established the solemnity of Christ the King in his encyclical *Quas Primas* as a reminder that there is only one King who reigns in the hearts of men, "of whose kingdom there shall be no end."[86] The kingship of Christ is a theme threaded through the Scriptures. He is the "King of Kings and Lord of Lords," who will reign forever (see Revelation 19:16).

This solemnity is on the last Sunday of the Church's liturgical calendar. The following Sunday is the First Sunday of Advent, marking the start of a new liturgical year. In these last days and weeks of the liturgical year, many liturgical texts and devotions focus on the end times. Due to its late addition to the Church's calendar, there are fewer devotional customs associated with this day, all of which tend to focus on the world to come.

Christus Vincit

The chant *Christus vincit* ("Christ conquers"), also known as the *Laudes regiae* ("Praise to the King") is a Catholic hymn fitting for this day. The call-and-response formula has a simple refrain of "*Christus vincit! Christus regnat! Christus imperat!*" or "Christ conquers! Christ reigns! Christ commands!" This refrain is followed by various invocations, including prayers for the long life of the emperor or the pope. This brief invocation has been handed down to us from ancient Rome, and is ubiquitous as a medieval inscription on coins, plates, and other objects. Charlemagne himself adopted this text following his coronation in the year 800.[87] The three short phrases were said to have powerful properties, including protection from evil, and for good weather. They are inscribed at the base of the obelisk in St. Peter's Square. An interesting fact is that a musical version of the *Christus vincit* is still used today by Vatican Radio.

Jesu Rex Admirabilis

A hymn text attributed to St. Bernard of Clairvaux (1090–1153) was originally used at Matins for the feast of the Holy Name of Jesus. It takes up the same themes as the *Christus vincit*: "O Jesu, King most wonderful, thou Conqueror renowned, thou sweetness most ineffable, in whom all joys are found!" This translation is by the nineteenth century hymnographer Edward Caswall. A choral version of this hymn is often credited to Palestrina, the great composer of polyphony from the Renaissance. Listen to music fitting for this feast day, including this piece and great classic hymns such as "Crown Him with Many Crowns."

Feast for a King

In many parts of the world, this solemnity falls during holidays centered around giving thanks for the harvest. Originally, Christ the King was celebrated at the end of October, but Pope Paul VI moved its celebration to the final Sunday of the liturgical year—which coincides with the time of Thanksgiving in the United States. These two feasts, one liturgical and one civic, have a harmonious balance in acknowledging our gratitude and our humility for the gifts bestowed on us by the Author of Creation.

Viva Cristo Rey

Around this time of the year, we also celebrate the feast day of Blessed Miguel Pro. Reading from the lives of the saints is a popular devotional practice in the Catholic family, and especially fitting in the month of November. Fr. Miguel Pro was a Mexican priest who carried out his ministry serving the faithful during the Mexican revolution, even while facing extreme religious persecution. After being falsely accused of another crime, he was sentenced to death and faced it fearlessly while forgiving his executioners. He is known for his devotion to Christ the King, proclaiming as he died, "*Viva Cristo Rey!*" ("Long live Christ the King!")

Most Sweet Jesus, Redeemer

On this feast day, a plenary indulgence is given for the public recitation of the prayer *Iesu dulcissime, Redemptor* ("Most Sweet Jesus, Redeemer"). This is an "Act of Dedication of the Human Race to Jesus Christ the King," in which the Church prays for the conversion of the world, unity, and peace among nations. This act is proclaimed publicly, meaning with a group of people, in a church or oratory, but can also be prayed in private devotion, receiving then a partial indulgence.[88]

Novena

In advance of this solemnity, a novena is prayed for the freedom of the Church and protection of Christ the King. There are various versions of the novena prayers. The prayer below is begun by saying one Our Father, one Hail Mary, and one Glory Be before praying the following:

> O Lord our God, Thou alone art the
> Most Holy King and Ruler of all nations.
> We pray to thee, Lord, in the great
> expectation of receiving from thee,
> O Divine King, mercy, peace, justice,
> and all good things.
> Protect, O Lord our King, our families,
> and the land of our birth.
>
> Guard us we pray, Most Faithful One.
> Protect us from our enemies and from
> thy just judgment.
> Forgive us, O Sovereign King,
> our sins against thee.
> Jesus, thou art a King of Mercy.
> We have deserved thy just judgment.
> Have mercy on us, Lord, and forgive us.
> We trust in thy Great Mercy. O most
> awe-inspiring King,
> We bow before Thee and pray:
> May thy reign, thy Kingdom,
> be recognized on earth. Amen.

ABOUT THE AUTHORS

Christopher Carstens is director of the Office for Sacred Worship of the Diocese of La Crosse. In addition, he is a visiting faculty member at the Liturgical Institute at the University of St. Mary of the Lake in Mundelein, Illinois, editor of the *Adoremus Bulletin*, and one of the voices on *The Liturgy Guys* podcast. Carstens is author of the books *A Devotional Journey into the Mass* and *Principles of Sacred Liturgy: Forming a Sacramental Vision*. He lives in Soldiers Grove, Wisconsin, with his wife and eight children.

Denis McNamara is an associate professor and executive director of the Center for Beauty and Culture at Benedictine College in Atchison, Kansas. He holds a bachelor's degree in the history of art from Yale University and a doctorate in architectural history from the University of Virginia, where his research focused on the study of ecclesiastical architecture of the nineteenth and twentieth centuries. He is the author of the books *Heavenly City: The Architectural Tradition of Catholic Chicago*, *Catholic Church Architecture and the Spirit of the Liturgy*, and *How to Read Churches: A Crash Course in Ecclesiastical Architecture*. He is a frequent presenter in academic and professional settings and is co-host of *The Liturgy Guys* podcast.

Alexis Kazimira Kutarna earned a master's degree in liturgy at the Liturgical Institute of the University of St. Mary of the Lake in Mundelein, Illinois. In addition, she holds master's and bachelor's degrees in music, and she is currently a candidate for the doctorate in liturgical studies, with a concentration in Church music, from the University of Vienna. Having served as a parish music and liturgy director, Alexis has worked with singers of all ages. She teaches courses on the liturgy and liturgical music at the University of St. Thomas in Houston, as well as a summer course for the St. Basil School of Gregorian chant. Currently, Alexis is the director of sacred music at Cathedral High School in Houston. Most important is her vocation as wife and mother to two little girls.

NOTES

1. Pius IX, *Ineffabilis Deus* (December 8, 1854).

2. Excerpts from prayers of the Mass are from the English translation of *The Roman Missal* © 2010 International Commission on English in the Liturgy.

3. Thomas Buffer and Bruce Horner, "The Art of the Immaculate Conception," *Marian Studies* 55 (2004), 184–185. This excellent piece provides interpretation of several versions of the Immaculate Conception and provided many of the interpretive ideas written here.

4. Homily of His Holiness Pope Francis on the 1050th Anniversary of the Baptism of Poland, Czestochowa, July 28, 2016.

5. Anna MacBride White and A. Norman Jeffares, *The Gonne-Yeats Letters 1893–1938* (Syracuse, NY: Syracuse University Press, 1994), 443.

6. Peter C. Phan, ed., *Directory on Popular Piety and Liturgy* (Collegeville, MN: Liturgical Press, 2005), 102.

7. Prosper Guéranger, *The Liturgical Year: Advent*, trans. Laurence Shepherd (1870), 403–404.

8. For an essay on the symbolic meaning of the painting, including the possibilities of the influence of Savonarola on Botticelli, see Rob Hatfield, "Botticelli's Mystic Nativity, Savonarola and the Millennium," *Journal of the Warburg and Courtauld Institutes* 58 (1995), 88–114.

9. *Catholic Household Blessings and Prayers* (Washington, DC: USCCB Publishing, 2020), 78–79.

10. *CHBP*, 81.

11. Ethel Urlin, *Festivals, Holy Days, and Saints' Days: A Study in Origins and Survivals in Church Ceremonies and Secular Customs* (London: Simpkin, Marshall, Hamilton, Kent & Co., 1915), 236–237.

12. Poetry by Robert Herrick, popularized by the musical setting of "What Sweeter Music" by the composer John Rutter in 1988.

13. The title *Theotokos* for Mary was defined at the Council of Ephesus in 431.

14. "The Easter Vigil in the Holy Night," *Roman Missal*, 3rd ed., 11.

15. Phan, *Directory on Popular Piety and Liturgy*, 114.

16. Phan, 116.

17. Urlin, 16–17.

18. Phan, 118.

19. *CHBP*, 88–91.

20. Phan, 219.

21. Pope Francis, apostolic letter *Patris Corde* (December 8, 2020), 7.

22. "A partial indulgence is granted to the faithful who invoke St. Joseph, spouse of the Blessed Virgin Mary, with a duly approved prayer." Apostolic Penitentiary, *The Manual of Indulgences* (Washington, DC: USCCB Publishing, 2006), 63–64.

23. Office of Readings for Friday of the Second Week of Advent.

24. Office of Readings for December 20.

25. With acknowledgment of the important interpretive contribution of the many articles of Jose Maria Salvador-Gonzalez, especially "The Annunciation in Fra Filippo Lippi: Interpreting Some Symbolic Variants," *Mirabilia Ars* 12 (2020).

26.   Phan, 197.

27.   Pius XII, Letter to the Archbishop of Manila, *Philippinas Insulas*: AAS 38 (1946), 419.

28.   Paul VI, *Marialis Cultus* (February 2, 1974), 41.

29.   From the hymn text "O Mystic Rose" by Fr. Mark A. Hebert, 2015.

30.   Paul Fieldhouse, *Food, Feasts, and Faith: An Encyclopedia of Food Culture in World Religions* (Santa Barbara, CA: ABC–CLIO, 2017), 35.

31.   Congregation for Divine Worship and the Disciple of the Sacraments, Circular Letter Concerning the Preparation and Celebration of the Easter Feasts, *Paschalis Sollemnitatis* (January 16, 1988), 85.

32.   Roman Missal, Easter Vigil, 21.

33.   Academic research on Raphael's *Resurrection* is scarce, but for an informative and speculative interpretation, see the entry by Kelly Bagdanov at kellybagdanov.com.

34.   Teresa of Avila, chap. 31 in *The Life of Teresa of Jesus* (New York: Benzinger Bros., 1904).

35.   *CHBP*, 125.

36.   Ukrainian Women's Association of Canada, *Ukrainian Daughters' Cookbook* (Saskatchewan: Ukrainian Women's Association of Canada, 1984).

37.   See William Saunders, *Celebrating a Holy Catholic Easter* (Charlotte, NC: TAN Books, 2020).

38.   United States Conference of Catholic Bishops, "What Is Easter?" Available at usccb.org/.

39.   Office of Readings for Wednesday of the Tenth Week in Ordinary Time.

40.   Office of Readings for Wednesday, Easter Week VI.

41.   Benedict XVI, *Jesus of Nazareth: Holy Week* (San Francisco: Ignatius, 2011), 82–83.

42.   Letter to Charles Wilson Peale, cited in Jules David Prown, "Benjamin West and the Use of Antiquity," *American Art* 10 (Summer 1996), 29.

43.   Jerry D. Meyer, "Benjamin West's Chapel of Revealed Religion: A Study in Eighteenth-Century Protestant Religious Art," *The Art Bulletin* 57 (June 1975), 254.

44.   St. John Chrysostom, Homily on the Ascension.

45.   *Aposticha* of Ascension Thursday Vespers, *Pentecostarion*.

46.   See Urlin, 113–114.

47.   Phan, 153.

48.   Gospel verse for Mass on Pentecost Sunday.

49.   Sermon by a sixth-century anonymous African author, Office of Readings from Saturday, Easter Week VII.

50.   Office of Readings for Pentecost.

51.   Romano Guardini, *Sacred Signs* (St. Louis: Pio Decimo Press, 1956), 30.

52.   Benedict XVI, apostolic exhortation *Verbum Domini* (September 30, 2010), 6.

53.   Dom Virgil Michel, *The Liturgy of the Church* (New York: Macmillan, 1937), 279.

54.   Guardini, 13.

55.   Phan, 157.

56.   Second Vatican Council, Instruction on Music in the Liturgy, *Musicam Sacram* (March 5, 1967), 5.

57.   Cited in Pope Benedict XVI's *Sacramentum Caritatis* (February 22, 2007), 70.

58.   Benedict XVI, homily given at the Mass of the Lord's Supper, 2009.

59.   Paul VI, *Lumen Gentium* (November 21, 1964), 11.

60.   *Sacramentum Caritatis*, 94.

61.   See Urlin, 152.

62.   Columba Marmion, *Christ and His Mysteries* (Colorado Springs: Zaccheus Press, 2008).

63.   J. Bainvel, "Devotion to the Sacred Heart of Jesus," *The Catholic Encyclopedia* (New York: Robert Appleton Company, 1910).

64.   Leo XIII, *Annum Sacrum* (May 25, 1889), 8, vatican.va/.

65.   See Leo XIII, encyclical on consecration to the Sacred Heart, *Annum Sacrum* (1899).

66.   Marmion, *Christ and His Mysteries*.

67.   For detailed investigations of the *Saint John Triptych*, see Barbara G. Lane, "Rogier's Saint John and Miraflores Altarpieces Reconsidered," *The Art Bulletin* 60 (December 1978), 655–672, and Victoria S. Reed, "Rogier van der Weyden's 'Saint John Triptych' for Miraflores and a Reconsideration of Salome," *Oud Holland* 115 (2001/2002), 1–14. Unless otherwise specified, interpretation of the painting's details is credited to these authors.

68.   From a sermon of St. Augustine for the Office of Readings on the Solemnity of the Nativity of St. John the Baptist (Sermon 293, 1–3: PL 38, 1327–1328).

69.   Adolf Adam, *The Liturgical Year: Its History and Its Meaning After the Reform of the Liturgy* (Collegeville, MN: Liturgical Press, 1981), 233.

70.   Phan, 225.

71.   Alfredo Tradigo, *Icons and Saints of the Eastern Orthodox Church* (Los Angeles: Getty Museum, 2006), 267.

72.   Pope Francis, homily given in St. Peter's Basilica, June 29, 2021.

73.   *Manual of Indulgences*, 1999, 33, §1.

74.   *Manual of Indulgences*, 1999, 20.

75.   Pius XII, *Munificentissimus Deus* (November 1, 1950), defining the dogma of the Assumption, citing St. Germanus of Constantinople, and read during the Office of Readings on this solemnity.

76.   Office of Readings for December 20.

77.   *Munificentissimus Deus*, 44.

78.   Preface for Mass of the day.

79.   *Lumen Gentium*, 59.

80.   Paul F. Bradshaw and Maxwell E. Johnson, *The Origins of Feasts, Fasts and Seasons in Early Christianity* (Collegeville, MN: Pueblo, 2011), 196.

81.   Urlin, 171.

82.   Excerpt from Olive Vivian, *Romance of Religion* (London: Forgotten Books, 2018).

83.   Entrance antiphon for Epiphany Mass during the day.

84.   Pius XI, encyclical letter *Quas Primas* (December 11, 1925), 28.

85.   Office of Readings for this solemnity.

86.   *Quas Primas*, 5, 7.

87.   Ernst Kantorowicz, *Laudes Regiae: A Study in Liturgical Acclamations and Medieval Ruler Worship* (Berkeley, CA: University of California Press, 1946).

88.   *Manual of Indulgences*, 2.

Foster **holiness** in all the **little moments** of Catholic family life

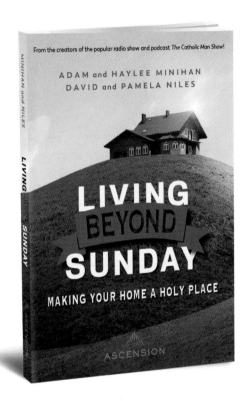

Our relationship with God is not supposed to stay within the walls of our parish church when we leave Sunday Mass. Instead, faith should transform our hearts, our families, and our homes into welcoming places to encounter Christ.

In ***Living Beyond Sunday: Making Your Home a Holy Place***, two married couples share what has helped them make their homes places of encounter with God—places where saints are being made.